Beyond
Catch & Release

Books by Paul Guernsey

Beyond Catch & Release

Angel Falls

Unhallowed Ground

Anthologies

*Upriver & Downstream: The Best Fly-Fishing & Angling Adventures
from the New York Times*

City Fishing

Children's Literature

Noah and the Ark

Beyond
Catch & Release

EXPLORING THE FUTURE OF FLY FISHING

Paul Guernsey

Photographs by Jim Rowinski

SKYHORSE PUBLISHING

www.skyhorsepublishing.com

10 9 8 7 6 5 4 3 2 1

Library of Congress Cataloging-in-Publication Data

Guernsey, Paul.
Beyond catch & release : exploring the future of fly fishing / Paul Guernsey.
    p. cm.
ISBN 978-1-61608-235-2 (alk. paper)
1. Fly fishing--Environmental aspects. 2. Fly fishing--Social aspects. I. Title.
II. Title: Beyond catch and release.
SH456.G76 2011
799.12'4--dc22

                         2010052685

Printed in China

For Maryann

And for our children, Nick and Katerina

Contents

Preface

What is a good angler?

Fly fishing is one of the most fulfilling ways of experiencing nature; it is one of the few activities that allows us to interact with the natural world as a participant rather than as a mere tourist. Because of this, people who fly fish belong to a privileged and extremely fortunate community. But with the privilege of angling and of belonging comes an important individual responsibility—the responsibility of each of us to be as good a fisherman or woman as we possibly can.

This is not, primarily, a matter of angling skills, although the acquisition, use, and sharing of fishing skills do play significant roles. Being a good angler involves much more than being able to catch fish when many other people cannot.

The anglers who are looked up to as the "best" by other sportsmen and women, in addition to being both knowledgeable and skillful, also invariably embody a universal set of ethics—shared values, respectful attitudes, and right behavior—toward the outdoors and the fish, wildlife, and people that inhabit them.

This ethical code of behavior is important to everyone who fishes, because it does not exist merely for its own sake. It is important because everything else depends on it. Without it, fishing would become merely a sport of conflict, and we would be able to take limited enjoyment or satisfaction from it. Eventually, there would come a day when fishing

11

itself would fade away—when anglers would lose access to many of their cherished fishing waters, the general public would turn against our beloved pastime, and the fish themselves would disappear, incrementally but thoroughly done away with by people and interests who care much more for convenience in every form as well as for manmade "assets" of the sort whose value can be readily measured and assessed to the final cent.

Fortunately, in every fishing community, good and ethical anglers abound—people who know how to treat others and who understand and actively defend the natural resources on which our sport depends against threats both small and large. Those who wish to become good anglers need only follow their example.

In my own life, I have been fortunate to have had the example of many fine anglers. Some of these men and women have written books and made videos and are famous in national or even international fishing circles. The majority, however, have never sought any sort of attention, are known only to a small group of fishing friends, family members, or clients, and are acclaimed only by a relative handful of local appreciators who understand their importance.

Although the following pages contain a few of my own fly-fishing experiences, *Beyond Catch & Release* is mostly the result of all I have learned from good anglers—fly fishers who at one time or another have been more knowledgeable, more perceptive, more patient, more positive, more courageous, more generous, more creative, or just much calmer than myself. In this book, it is with the wisdom and knowledge so generously shared with me by these men and women that I hope to illuminate some of our sport's possible paths through the complications of the twenty-first century. It promises to be an interesting journey—one that requires anglers as a group to remain cohesive as well as adaptable in an environment of rapid social and environmental change, while at the same time never losing touch with the centuries-old traditions that both guide and define us.

We can begin to map our way forward by taking a respectful but critical look at both the traditions and the history of our sport, as well as by agreeing, at least in general, on what makes up the ethic of a good fisherman in today's world. Once we've arrived at that rough consensus, we can then discuss how best to refine and redefine some of our beliefs, habits, and attitudes in order to meet the challenges of *tomorrow's* world.

I believe that if we are successful, fly fishing will endure throughout this century and perhaps long into the next, prospering and even contributing, at least in a modest way, to the greater well-being of the earth's waters, wildlife, and people.

—Paul Guernsey
December 2010

Beyond
Catch & Release

1

The Tradition
of Fly Fishing

You that can angle and catch fish
for your pleasure . . .

I n the beginning, people fished because they were hungry. Fish
populations were thought to be unlimited, and the only responsibility
a fisherman had was to his growling stomach, and to the growling
stomachs of his family, tribe, or village. The only rule he recognized was
the one that told him that he better not allow fishermen from other
families, tribes, or villages to get in his way.

After a time, however, some European anglers began to play with
their food. They decided that fishing was fun, they made a game of it,
and they called it "sport."

As with any sport, a certain level of sportsmanship was expected of
the sportsmen and, as with any game, rules were needed in order to keep
the players from spoiling their own enjoyment. Although writings about
all sorts of fishing, including fly fishing, go back well over a thousand

years, the first written angling "code" appeared four years after the time of Columbus's first voyage with the publication of a longish essay entitled "A Treatyse of Fysshynge wyth an Angle," or "A Treatise of Fishing with an Angle." Of unknown authorship, but popularly attributed to an English nun—a prioress named Dame Juliana Berners—the "Treatise" has mostly to do with tackle-making and fishing techniques for the English countryside, and its author was too practical to restrict herself exclusively to trout as a quarry or fly fishing as a method. In fact, the author considered her advice to be so dangerously effective in the taking of all species of fish that, rather than publishing it as an inexpensive pamphlet, she included it in the large and relatively pricey *Book of St. Albans* specifically to make it unaffordable to the riffraff—or as she termed them, "idle persons."

While most of the tackle advice in the "Treatise" is now of only historical interest, the final portion, in which the author offers rules on manners, conservation, and landowner relations, is every bit as valid today as it was five hundred years ago:

> Here follows the order made to all those who shall have the understanding of this aforesaid treatise and use it for their pleasures.
>
> You that can angle and catch fish for your pleasure, as the aforesaid treatise teaches and shows you: I charge and require you in the name of all noble men that you do not fish in any poor man's private water: as his pond: stew: or other necessary things to keep fish in without his license and good will.
>
> Nor that you use not to break any man's engines lying in their weirs and in other places due to them. Nor to take the fish away that is taken in them. For after a fish is taken in a man's trap, if the trap is laid in the public waters: or else in such waters as he hires, it is his own personal property.

And if you take it away, you rob him: which is a right shameful deed for any gentle man to do, that the thieves and robbers do, who are punished for their evil deeds by the neck and otherwise when they can be found and captured.

And also if you do in like manner as this treatise shows you: you will have no need to take other men's fish, while you will have enough of your own catching, if you wish to work for them.

It will be a true pleasure to see the fair, bright, shining-scaled fishes deceived by your crafty means and drawn upon the land. Also, I charge you, that you break no man's hedges in going about your sports: nor open any man's gates but that you shut them again.

Also, you must not use this aforesaid artful sport for covetousness to increasing or saving of your money only, but principally for your solace and to promote the health of your body and especially of your soul.

For when you propose to go on your sports in fishing, you will not desire greatly many persons with you, which might hinder in letting you at your game.

And then you can serve God devoutly by earnestly saying your customary prayers. And thus doing, you will eschew and avoid many vices, such as idleness, which is the principal cause to induce man to many other vices, as is right well known.

Also, you must not be too greedy in catching your said game as taking too much at one time, which you may easily do if you do as this present treatise shows you in every point. Which could easily be the occasion of destroying your own sport and other men's also.

And when you have a sufficient mess you should covet no more at that time. Also you shall help yourself to nourish the game in all that you may, and to destroy all such things as are devourers of it. And all those that do as this rule shall have the blessing of God and St. Peter.

Which he grants them that with his precious blood he bought.

And so that this present treatise should not come into the hands of every idle person who would desire it if it were printed alone by itself and put in a little pamphlet, therefore I have compiled it in a greater volume of diverse books concerning gentle and noble men, to the end that the aforesaid idle persons which should have but little measure in the said sport of fishing should not by this means utterly destroy it.

Over the many centuries that separate the "Treatise" author's time from ours, self-appointed angling authorities on two continents have occasionally tried to add to her injunctions concerning sportsmanship. One highly successful amendment—or at least, one that has caught on with many of us, and which the author herself probably would never have considered—is the conceit that fly fishing is the "highest and best" form of recreational angling. Another idea that took firm root, but which we may be in the process of losing, is the elevation of trout and salmon as the "most worthwhile," if not the "only truly worthwhile," gamefish. Then, of course, there's the concept of catch-and-release angling, which I am fairly certain the author of the "Treatise" would have recognized as a form of "idleness."

Other proposed strictures, though they may have been popular for a time in some rarified circles, never quite survived as tenets in our accepted canon of traditions. A few that leap readily to mind are the idea that an angler should always cast *upstream,* the admonition that when the angler did cast, it should always be to a feeding fish, *never* merely to a promising bit of water, the opinion that wading was rude and that fishing should be done from the bank and, lastly, the oppressive commandment that dry-fly fishing somehow superseded all other methods of fly fishing, and had therefore become the only acceptable way of going about the sport of angling. All these concepts enjoyed something of a vogue on the nineteenth-century English chalkstreams before fading away almost as completely as the notion that proper angling attire should consist of ties, tweed coats, long dresses, and bonnets.

In spite of our sport's traditional and ethical evolution, however, and with the one exception of an implied advisory to kill all fish-eating predators—we know better than that now—the rules that still seem to matter the most today are the same ones the "Treatise" set forth, and which we moderns could probably distill to:

Be considerate of other anglers, landowners, and the general public.
Respect your quarry.
Do what you can to protect fish and fish habitat.
Take precautions for the sake of your own health and safety.
Help and teach others.
Enjoy your time outdoors.

The only thing beyond this that's needed is a little friendly, ongoing conversation among twenty-first-century anglers on how best to follow these commonsense guidelines in a time and an environment as increasingly complicated as our own.

2

Americans (Re)Learn
the Need for Rules

. . . which is a right shameful deed for any gentle man to do, that the thieves and robbers do, who are punished for their evil deeds . . .

During the 100 years after the "Treatise" was written, the earliest North American anglers began abandoning a European continent that was full of rules governing the taking of fish—the gentle suggestions in the "Treatise" as well as a raft of harshly enforced restrictions serving to protect the sporting "rights" of the aristocracy—and sailed to a New World where there were few limits on the exploitation of natural resources. American fish, fowl, and other game seemed inexhaustible, and each person was entitled to fish and hunt where and when he or she wanted, using whatever method was most convenient, and to harvest—and sell—as much as he or she saw fit. The sense of freedom must have been intoxicating.

Over the following three centuries, even as sportsmen on this continent were developing a uniquely American tradition of angling, we began to slowly relearn the hard, painful, and inescapable fact that fish are a finite and often fragile resource—that too much killing of fish by too many anglers or by using destructive methods inevitably leads to fewer and smaller fish, that dams would almost invariably decimate runs of such river-spawning ocean fish as salmon and shad, and that raw sewage, industrial pollution, and the stripping of timber from watersheds would render once-productive waters entirely unsuitable for trout and other fish.

For a while, however, these were easy lessons to ignore, as American anglers always had the possibility of moving on to less-pressured waters, which is what many of them did. During the decades following the Civil War, anglers from Boston and New York began riding the new railroads to Maine, the Adirondacks, even to Yellowstone, where they often fished with the same lack of restraint, sometimes involving appalling waste as well as greed, that had already emptied the streams and lakes closer to home. For just one example, after Maine's Rangeley Lakes region had opened as a sporting destination in the mid-1800s, anglers regularly caught more trophy-size, five- to ten-pound brook trout than they could possibly eat or afford to have mounted. But rather than quitting for the day when they had enough, or at least releasing a few fish, they typically carried the "surplus" back to camp, where it briefly went on display, sometimes for an impressive "sporting" photograph, before being tossed into a ditch. Daily catch competitions at Rangeley area sporting camps provided additional incentive for the slaughter.

In 1901, when Maine belatedly got around to imposing a legal limit on brook trout—25 pounds of trout per day per person—it was too little, and had come far too late. Wasteful fishing, in combination with several other manmade environmental problems including the introduction by humans of nonnative fish species, had already all but wiped out Maine's race of giant brook trout.

But Maine was far from unique: Similar tragedies were unfolding all across the continent at around the same time. By the time Maine had been discovered as a sport-fishing destination, industrial dams throughout New England had already begun choking off the great, now extirpated, runs of Atlantic salmon, and New York anglers were busy fishing out the sea-run brook trout streams of Long Island, the lakes of the Adirondacks, and the Catskill Mountain rivers—which were also being heavily damaged by deforestation and industrial water pollution. Meanwhile, in the Southeast, intensive logging and farming in the Appalachian watersheds were causing the destruction by siltation of fish habitat at the southern end of the brook trout's range and, across the continent, post–Civil War settlers in the pristine Yellowstone River region were setting about killing and selling almost unimaginable numbers of wild animals and wild fish. The slaughter of the buffalo is of course a well-known, and now cautionary, American story; fewer Americans know about or mourn the area's millions of cutthroat trout, which were market-fished so intensively with dynamite, nets, and other destructive methods that twentieth-century fisheries managers would soon seek to repopulate relatively empty cutthroat habitat with alien rainbow and brown trout.

Finally, however, it became all too apparent that there would not always be pristine trout water beyond the next hill. While newly conscious sportsmen could do little to combat the industrial and agricultural causes of fish habitat degradation, they could at least begin making an attempt to moderate their own behavior, and that of other anglers. Anglers in some areas began banding together in order to set restrictions on fishing tactics as well as on the numbers of fish that could be taken.

The country's first real, concerted conservation efforts took place in the late 1800s and involved the establishment of private clubs that restricted access to paying members. By the 1870s, fishing clubs, with paid watchmen and "no trespassing" signs, had already been established on Long Island and were springing up all over New York's famed Catskills streams in order to preserve the dwindling fish, as well as the fishing privileges of the club members. The club concept was nearly irresistible to those who not only were concerned about the decline of the fisheries but who could also afford to buy in, and by the turn of the twentieth century, the idea had spread as far as California's McCloud River, which was esteemed for its rainbow trout fishing.

Private clubs, of course, meant shutting out most of the public, and the regular run of fishermen often reacted with anger, as well as occasional violence. Gradually, however, a more satisfactory remedy was reached: Anglers' groups first prevailed on their county governments to pass such regulations as outlawing fishing on Sunday, banning commercial fishing for trout, and restricting legal fishing equipment to rods and lines. Gone, at last and for good, were the old net-and-dynamite days. Then fishermen began to lobby their state legislatures to enact bag limits and other laws, as well as to establish "fish commissions" with the authority to enforce the new regulations. State game wardens, with the full power of the government behind them, began appearing on streams and lakes across the country.

Slowly but inevitably, as the world moved deeper into the twentieth century, the rules governing sport fishing became stricter and more sophisticated. Most states began to require anglers to release fish that were under a certain size. Places like Maine, whose initial, generous daily trout quotas were measured in pounds, finally reduced those limits to numbers of individual fish that could be kept. Eventually, professional managers throughout the country would be intensively managing freshwater sport fisheries in an attempt to concoct an effective formula of laws and practices for each of our individual waters. A few examples include: stocking rivers and lakes with hatchery fish; *discontinuing* the stocking of hatchery fish when it proved to be ineffective or worse; closing spawning waters to angling during spawning season; banning such gear as treble hooks in some places, seasons, and situations; imposing strict artificial-lures-only and even catch-and-release-only regulations in others; and, perhaps the most sophisticated rule-book remedy to date, imposing "slot limits," under which anglers must release all fish under one certain length and *over* another in order to conserve the breeding population.

Following the Rules

The states have been managing and controlling fisheries for so long now that many of us are unaware that the need for rules was first recognized and acted upon by anglers themselves, who banded together to demand that their governments impose regulations and undertake enforcement. The states are merely continuing to do what we asked them to do a long time ago.

In other words, just as the waters are ours and the fish are ours, the laws belong to us as well, much as we might quibble with some of them. Without them, none of us would fish at all because gamefish would exist only in the most remote locations—and those beleaguered holdouts would be rapidly dwindling in number.

But rules only work if they are followed, and followed equally by everyone. Each of us owes it to other anglers and to the fishing resource itself to obey our angling regulations.

It goes almost without saying that in order to obey the regulations, an angler first needs to know what those regulations *are*. That means learning the regulations ourselves rather than relying on other anglers to inform us about any restrictions.

Almost everywhere, a free copy of the state rule book comes with the purchase of a fishing license; it is the obligation of each of us to become familiar not only with the general regulations, but also with any specific regulations governing angling conduct on the individual waters we intend to fish.

Nor should anglers tolerate or ignore rule breaking or poaching by others. If the infraction we witness is a small one, and we determine that it is being made out of sheer ignorance—if someone obviously just did not read their regulations—then we might decide to say something to the rule breaker in a friendly, or a least nonconfrontational, manner.

However, when we see serious violations occurring in clear disregard for the law—fishing in a closed area, exceeding the legal bag limit, killing fish in a catch-and-release-only zone, keeping fish smaller (or larger) than allowed by law, or using bait in an area that is restricted to artificial lures—it is better not to try to handle the situation ourselves. We should instead collect any useful information such as automobile license plate numbers and descriptions of the people and vehicles involved, and report the behavior to the state fish and game department as soon as possible. Nothing less than the future of the fishery depends on our vigilance and willingness to take action, because a successful rule breaker will not only continue to break the rules, but he will take his friends along with him the next time he goes fishing.

If state fishing regulations have a fault, it is often that they allow anglers to take more fish than is healthful for the fisheries. This is in part because the people who make the regulations are hired by politicians, and politicians often make decisions based on whatever is likely to make them popular—or at least keep them out of controversy. It is important therefore for ethical, conservation-minded anglers to join forces in order to advocate for ever more effective fishing regulations. The loudest voices heard by politicians and fisheries managers often are the ones calling for more generous bag limits, and greater reliance on the stocking of hatchery fish.

We need to make sure that ours are just as loud.

3

To Catch-and-Release—and Beyond

Also, you must not be too greedy in catching your said game as taking too much at one time . . . [w]hich could easily be the occasion of destroying your own sport and other men's also.

Although I have seen many fly fishermen kill trout, the last such killing I witnessed took place so long ago I have trouble remembering where or when it happened. Catch-and-release has become such a near-universal reflex among fly anglers that the sacrifice of a gamefish has become a rare, even shocking, event.

In fact, rather than dying at the hands of its captor as it almost inevitably would have done a mere few decades ago, nearly every trout of above-average size is now treated as an honored guest: Greeted with warmth and cheer, its immediate needs immediately attended to, it soon finds itself posing for photographs in the affectionate embrace of its host. Then, following further celebratory ritual, it is given a good rest before being sent on its way with a sincere invitation to return.

I am sure there are many younger fly fishers who, if they did not get their start in the generally less genteel world of spin fishing, have *never* seen a trout intentionally killed. Meanwhile, many of the rest of us who once had fish blood on our hands have forgotten the intense psychological transformation we had to undergo in order to arrive at what we like to view as our current state of enlightenment.

But before the catch-and-release revolution took hold, anglers typically did not allow themselves to count a fish as truly "caught" unless it was either dead, or kicking its way to death in the bottom of a fish bag or creel. And although "advanced" fishermen would often boast of "throwing back" a few fish even before they had filled their bag limit, the released fish were almost always the smaller ones rather than those of breeding size, which, if they were returned alive to the water, would not only be discounted by other anglers and by society at large, but also considered to have been "wasted." That glow of virtue at releasing a few smaller fish could not ignite unless the angler had also proven his adequacy by catching, possessing, and displaying a few larger ones.

In fact, often there was intense "killing pressure" on anglers from nonfishing family members and friends as well as from other fishermen. Anglers returning from a river were invariably asked, "So, where are all the fish?" and, whenever it came up in conversation that a person was a dedicated angler, one of the first comments always was, "Well then, your freezer must be full of fish!"

An angler who returned home empty-handed was frequently looked upon as either a bad fisherman—and mocked as such—or a liar who was using fishing as a beard for some other, darker vice.

Gradually, however—and the change was able to occur only with a lot of mutual moral support among the growing ranks of "eccentric" catch-and-release anglers—we were able to make a shift in our personal definitions of both "catching" and "possessing." After a while, a kill was no longer the inevitable culmination of a legitimate catch, and the possession of a good fish, while still important, no longer meant permanent ownership, unto the frying pan. Instead, we—the fly-fishing tribe—replaced the literal sacrifice of the fish with ritual: We began to allow ourselves to claim legitimate possession by netting them, by touching them, by fussing over them, by displaying them in all their vital beauty to our fishing companions—and ultimately, by watching them swim away.

Cameras, rather than creels, became the indispensable streamside accessory, and the release, rather than the death, of the fish became the emotionally satisfying object of our game.

As newly ordained catch-and-release anglers, not only did we applaud one another for our greatness of spirit, but we gave one another moral support with which to confront our non-angling critics. Together we scripted and shared such standard homilies as, "A golfer doesn't eat the golf ball when he's done playing, so I don't need to eat the fish," and, more usefully, "I want to catch that same fish again, after it grows another inch or two."

A lot of non-anglers never really understood any of this. But most, after a time, eventually shrugged, lessened their talk of freezers and frying pans, and began to leave us largely alone.

Catch-and-release has now been the norm for several decades. In fact, most of us who as individual anglers went through the internal struggle over what it meant to "catch" a fish have forgotten not only how hard that adjustment was, but we barely remember having gone through it in the first place.

More importantly and more seriously, catch-and-release has become such a reflexive action that we hardly think about it at all anymore. Most of us barely give a thought to why we return living fish to the water. But the reason is important.

The great fly-fishing explorer and innovator, Lee Wulff, is widely credited with having launched catch-and-release angling in the United States when he famously declared in his 1939 book, *Lee Wulff's Handbook of Freshwater Fishing*, that, "Gamefish are too valuable to be caught only once," and "The fish you release is your gift to another angler and, remember, it may have been someone's similar gift to you."

But Wulff was only giving public voice to the beliefs of a small but deeply convinced group of fisheries managers, scientists, and fishermen

who had been advocating for anglers to release more of their catch. He was certainly far from the first observer to point out that trout streams could not take the harvesting pressure we were putting on them, and that something had to give.

Fishing writers from the time of the "Treatise" onward had been admonishing anglers not to be "greedy," and to limit their catch—by which they usually only meant leaving the stream after they had caught enough fish for a substantial supper. And by the turn of the twentieth century, a lonely handful of farsighted pioneers, including American dry-fly popularizer Theodore Gordon, were even suggesting that anglers release a few of their larger fish as a conservation measure.

While some anglers during the first half of the last century actually took this advice to heart, many others were unable to adjust their notions of "catching." When World War II came and then ended, a newly affluent and mobile American public aggressively renewed its interest in outdoor recreation, and an angling innovation, the spinning rod, "democratized" fishing by making it easy. Suddenly, there was more fishing pressure than ever—so much, in fact, that even greatly reduced bag limits could not keep trout in the nation's waters.

By this time, some fisheries managers already knew that the planting of hatchery fish was not the answer. Research conducted as far back as the 1930s indicated that stocking in streams containing wild fish tended to *reduce* rather than increase overall fish populations and result in *smaller*, rather than larger, fish. Even though hatchery trout were ill-suited for survival in the wild, during their brief in-stream existence they nonetheless managed to interfere with both reproduction and survival for the fish that had been born there.

Scientific evidence notwithstanding, states responded to the boom in demand for fish by expanding fish hatcheries and pumping increasing numbers of pale, mass-produced fish into their rivers and lakes. While this artificial and ultimately self-defeating solution satisfied a lot of anglers, it was far from satisfactory for those of us who not only were aware of the drawbacks, but who had caught wild fish, who possessed what conservation pioneer Aldo Leopold called "a refined taste in natural objects," and who knew how a real trout was supposed to look, behave, and fit into its natural environment.

On the remaining heavily fished streams still containing fish that were native, or that at least were wild and naturally reproducing, the choices were stark: Get used to catching ever-fewer and ever-smaller fish; quit fishing altogether; or keep fishing, but quit taking the fish.

Starting in the 1950s, the practice of catch-and-release—largely voluntary, and originally called "fishing for fun" in the early days—finally began to gain some real momentum. In 1959, a group of sixteen Michigan anglers started meeting to share their concerns about their state's fish-stocking policy; the group eventually blossomed into Trout Unlimited, a powerful, national conservation organization that continues to work to conserve native and wild fish and fish habitat across the country.

The mid-1960s brought the rise of the Federation of Fly Fishers, another national conservation-minded network of fishing clubs. Other groups were forming as well.

These new organizations were part of a growing movement, and "fishing for fun," as it spread and became mandatory on some of the harder-fished waters of many states, began to acquire the weightier label that it carries today. (The term "catch-and-release" may have been coined in the early 1960s by Richard Stroud, a biologist working for the tackle industry-funded Sport Fishing Institute, who reportedly did not care for the earlier, more frivolous-sounding, phrase.)

A huge milestone came in 1973, when fisheries managers in Yellowstone National Park, one of the nation's premier angling destinations, were forced to impose strict catch-and-release regulations in order to prevent the park's storied rivers from being completely emptied of trout. By the late 1980s and early 1990s, when technological advances in angling equipment enabled the popularization of saltwater fly fishing, "C&R" had become so thoroughly engrained in the angling ethic that most saltwater fly rodders released their "new" and relatively abundant quarry without even giving their actions a second thought.

To further abbreviate a lengthy and complicated history, catch-and-release angling came about and caught on because it was a practical and effective fisheries management tool, *and for no other reason.*

However, as the practice ceased to be questioned among anglers and its acceptance became nearly universal, it quickly began to gather the adornment of mythology—perhaps even of theology. Many anglers began to view the release of a fish as an act of generosity toward that individual fish—they were sparing its life for life's own sake—rather than strictly as an action necessary for the preservation of a fish population. A lot of us who released large fish ended up feeling good about ourselves in ways that had nothing to do with the science of fisheries conservation. For just one example, during the 1990s, as a fishing magazine editor, I began to notice that a growing number of fly fishers with literary ambitions were writing and seeking to publish fanciful fictional stories in which a newly released fish "appeared to wink"—a neat trick, as fish have no eyelids—"seemed to wave its tail," or even transformed itself into a voluptuous mermaid or the reincarnation of a departed loved one by way of expressing gratitude for not being killed by its captor.

Rather than viewing our actions as being merely those of prudent conservationists, we catch-and-release fly fishers were seeing ourselves as lifesaving heroes.

Most of this was just good, clean, imaginative fun that only added enjoyment to our sport, the way Santa Claus adds to the merriment of Christmas. And it was far preferable to our former habit of filling bags and baskets with our precious wild fish.

However, the whole thing becomes not so harmless when we heroes begin seeing others as villains, when we insist that everyone else—spin, bait, and fly anglers alike—also view catch-and-release in moral rather than managerial terms.

On many waters, anglers are still allowed to "take" a few fish. Particularly on rivers where most of the fish have been stocked and little natural reproduction is taking place, it is silly as well as counterproductive to become publicly indignant over the legal taking of a fish that was put there in the first place primarily as quarry for anglers. While many of us might prefer to release that fish in hopes of catching it again, and some of us might even feel it is "wrong" to end the life of even a stocked fish, we should allow our preferences and feelings to guide our own actions, and not demand that they guide those of others. It is important to keep in mind that a licensed angler who is permitted by regulation to keep a fish, and who elects to do so, is within his legal as well as his moral rights. He or she has done nothing unethical or wrong.

There are even places—many Western brook trout waters, for instance—where a certain amount of catch-and-kill among a naturally reproducing fish population is actually good for the fishery, or at least does little harm.

That is not to say, however, that if we think the regulations on a particular water are not sufficiently restrictive, and are allowing harm to be done to the wild fish population, we shouldn't ask, even insist, that our fish and game departments change those regulations. Nor does it mean that we shouldn't, in a friendly manner, encourage one another to release fish when we think it is in the best biological interest of the fishery to do so.

But I think that, in some cases, we fly fishers let emotions get in the way of common sense regarding conservation, and that can hurt our interests in the long run. We are, after all, a minority of the fishing population, and we will always need allies beyond our own small fraternity in the ongoing fight to protect fish habitat and native fish, and to keep our waters clean and open to public access. We need the help of other outdoorsmen, and we require the goodwill of everyone who fishes, even those who use other types of gear than we prefer, and who might view individual fish with less sentimentality than we do.

In other words, in all cases it is the resource as a whole that is important, not the individual fish, and we can't afford to create unnecessary bad feelings among other types of recreationalists by appearing elitist, humorless, inflexible, or intolerant.

We fly fishers can accomplish the most for the future of fish and the sport of fishing by setting a good—and good-natured—onstream example as well as by exercising conservation leadership of only the friendliest and most inclusive sort. We need to lower the barriers between ourselves and other types of recreational anglers, not make them higher.

Nor should we fool ourselves into thinking that by invariably practicing catch-and-release, we are doing all we need to do to ensure the future of our sport. C&R by itself is far from enough, because here in the complicated twenty-first century, the actions of anglers themselves are no longer the primary threat to angling. Instead, fish and fishing waters face a host of serious threats, including but not limited to habitat loss and degradation; exotic pests, diseases, and fish species; warming water temperatures brought about by climate change; and the private enclosure of rivers and lakes to which there was once public access.

While one of the main problems in the early to mid-twentieth century was that of too many anglers pressuring our waters, *it has always been anglers who naturally cared the most about fish and fish habitat and who have fought the hardest to defend them.* As we go further into the twenty-first century, it will likely be the *declining* number of anglers that spells the most trouble for our cause.

Over the coming decades, we anglers will need to look far beyond catch-and-release to preserve the waters and aquatic wildlife we cherish. We will need to find creative ways to enlist new anglers and conservationists, to preserve habitat, and to nurture native species. We will have to come up with new solutions for reducing our own impact on fresh and salt waters alike.

Perhaps most importantly, part of being a good and ethical fly fisher has now come to include being an ambassador to other anglers, including other *types* of anglers, as well as to other outdoor recreationalists and to the public at large.

In short, twenty-first-century anglers have plenty of opportunities for improving the enjoyment of their sport through their interactions with institutions, groups, and individuals, as well as with the natural world as a whole. These relationships include but are not limited to those involving anglers and:

The Fish
Waters, Woods, and Mountains
Other Fishermen and Women
The Next Generation of Anglers
The Public at Large
Themselves
The Future of Fly Fishing and Outdoor Recreation

Each of these relationships deserves a closer look, and a much more detailed explanation.

4

The Fish

**It will be a true pleasure to see the fair, bright, shining-scaled fishes deceived
by your crafty means and drawn
upon the land.**

There is a cost to a fish in being caught, even if it is promptly released. While a feeding fish is steadily adding energy to its personal survival account, a fish that is hooked and fought is forced to make a withdrawal. In addition, acids and other waste products accumulate in the muscles of a struggling fish, potentially reaching lethal levels if the fight goes on for too long or if conditions are especially stressful.

A released fish may not resume feeding for a time—sometimes for up to a day—which further effects its long-term well-being.

Generally, when the fight on the angler's part is an efficient one and the subsequent release is prompt, the expenditure in calories and recovery time is relatively small. Nonetheless, it does take at least a tiny toll on the fish's ability to compete with others of its species, to reproduce and to make it through another winter. And repeatedly being caught and released, especially during hot summer conditions under which the water contains less oxygen than at other times, can have a serious effect on the health of a fish.

An angler should be aware of these facts, and should try to minimize the price that a fish has to pay for having been caught by treating it with care, respect, and concern for its survival. In addition to being a living creature, each fish is part of a natural resource, and ethical catch-and-release anglers take pains not to "use up" more of it than is absolutely necessary to hook it, bring it to hand, and return it to the water.

Ethical Fishing, and Ethical Fishing Gear

Temperature

Water temperature is perhaps the largest factor in determining whether a caught trout lives or dies. The warmer the water, the less oxygen it contains. In addition, fish have a much easier time clearing the toxins from their muscles when the water is cooler.

Not all heat-affected fish will die in your hands; some will die after you release them and they swim away.

It is a fine idea, especially on waters where trout reproduce naturally and are not just playthings stocked by the state, to carry a thermometer in the summer and check the water temperature from time to time. Rainbows and browns begin to be stressed beyond endurance when caught in water temperatures above 70 degrees Fahrenheit (21 Celsius). Adult brook trout, for their part, often have difficulty surviving for long at those temperatures *even when they're not being stressed.* It seems prudent, therefore, to quit fishing for brookies when the water temperature approaches the mid-sixties Fahrenheit (about 18 Celsius).

Bass, of course, are popularly known as "warmwater" fish, and are much more resilient than trout, even when water temperatures climb into the high seventies.

Hooks: Barbed vs. Barbless

The hooking of a fish starts, of course, with the hook. A barbless hook—which usually means a hook whose barb has been mashed flat by an angler using pliers or forceps—is more easily removed than a barbed hook, which makes releasing a fish go more quickly. In addition, much of the physical trauma that goes along with removing a barbed hook from living tissue is avoided.

A handful of barbed-hook proponents argue that a barbless hook penetrates more deeply, and that the wound caused by a barbless hook tends to enlarge as the hooked fish fights against the angler, a problem that does not occur when the barb is up and holding fast. While there might be some truth to this claim—actual research is scarce—most experienced anglers believe that the advantages of a speedy, barbless release far outweigh whatever benefits barbed hooks might offer. In fact, it seems difficult these days even to find an angler who will put in a good word for barbs on hooks, or admit to using them.

A Short, Fierce, and Honorable Fight

Although most of the skill in angling has to do with presenting the fly in a way that convinces the fish to eat it, much of the emotional drama comes from the fight. However, it is important for the well-being of the fish that the fight not go on for any longer than is necessary.

The longer a fish is forced to struggle, the more tired it gets and the more time it requires to recover from having been caught. A thoroughly exhausted fish, its muscles depleted of oxygen and loaded with lactic acid and other waste products of overexertion, stands a chance of not recovering at all, or of being grabbed by a predator in its weakened condition.

An efficient fight involves applying close to as much pressure on the fish as the tippet is meant to withstand, and applying it with a fly rod appropriate for the species and size of the fish. Light rods for larger fish are sporting *only if they don't prolong the fight.* If a rod lacks the backbone to bring the fish to the angler within a reasonable amount of time, then it is the wrong tool for the job.

In addition, the angler should always choose the strongest possible tippet for any particular fishing situation. An unnecessarily delicate tippet that encourages an angler to prolong the fight is bad for the fish and diminishes, rather than increases, the level of sport the angler experiences.

Handling and Unhooking Fish without Hurting Them

For the fish, the trauma continues even after the fight is finished. It still has a hook—in its mouth, hopefully!—which must be removed, after which it requires anywhere from a few seconds to a few minutes of recovery time before it swims away. In fact, depending on the actions of the angler, the period between landing and release can be just as stressful, or even more so, than the battle that preceded it.

In most cases, the angler who handles least handles best. Often, following a fast and relatively stress-free fight, it is barely necessary even to touch the fish in order to release it—a barbless fly hooked into the front part of the mouth more often than not will detach with a little twist of the angler's thumb and forefinger, or with just a bit of help from the forceps or hemostats that every angler should carry.

If the fly refuses to come out, however, then it becomes necessary to handle the fish. A grip, firm but light as possible, in combination with the deft use of the forceps, usually removes a barbless hook in short order. Turning a fish onto its back temporarily disorients it, and often seems to calm it for the amount of time it takes to remove the fly. When handling fish, anglers should always take care to avoid touching their delicate eyes and gills.

It is important to remember that every second a fish is out of water is a second during which that fish is suffocating. The release should be done underwater if possible; if not, the fish should be held in the air for as little time as possible.

If you are planning to photograph a fish, make sure everything is set up and ready for the photo *before you take the fish out of the water.* Then, when taking the photo, hold the fish as close to the water as possible in order to prevent injury in case it flips out of your grasp, and be careful to support its belly with your hands. If you are concerned about a good fish escaping before you get your "hero" shot, it is far healthier for the fish if you leave the fly and leader in its mouth as a temporary "leash" than it is to clamp the poor thing in a literal death grip.

Once you've taken your picture, return the fish to the water as quickly as possible. And please keep in mind that it is not necessary to photograph every fish you catch.

Also important is for the release always to take place in the shallows or other area of light current, as a strong current can sweep and tumble a tired fish to its doom before it has had a chance to recover its strength. Ideally, the fish will have a quiet spot where it can rest, facing upstream, until it feels ready to swim away on its own.

An angler who has any doubts about a fish's ability to control its movements in the current has the obligation of caring for it until it is ready to go. Once the hook has been removed, the angler needs to gently cradle the fish in his or her hands with its head facing upstream until it shows signs of being strong enough to leave. Light pressure from a finger or thumb on the fish's lower jaw will open the mouth a bit, allowing more water, and therefore more oxygen, to flow across the fish's gills, thereby shortening the recovery time.

A fish that is feeling strong enough to leave your care will usually signal this by "kicking" a few times in your hands. When this happens, the angler can loosen his or her grip even further and wait for the fish to swim. A healthy fish will usually try to swim upstream before beginning to drift backward with the current. Often you will see it settle to the bottom, head still facing upstream, to rest for a while on its own. If a released fish begins to roll or shows any other signs that the current has the best of it, the angler should try to recover the fish in order to rest it for a while longer.

Some anglers will try to hurry a release when faced with such distractions as rising fish, a hatch that is tapering off, or a sun that is setting on the angler's fishing day. But, for the ethical angler, the only important fish is the one he or she has caught and is caring for. Only when that fish has been safely returned to the water can the angler resume thinking about all the fish that have *not* been caught.

For salt and freshwater fish alike, there are a variety of "release tools" other than forceps and pliers that can make the job go more smoothly and quickly. Most of these are worth trying. One that I have used successfully is called the Ketchum Release—essentially a short plastic tube with a narrow opening or slot down the length of it, which has been fitted to a handle. When it's time to send a fish on its way, the tippet passes through the slot and into the tube, after which the angler merely slides the tube down the tippet until it meets the fly. A little flex of the wrist at that point usually frees the hook. For larger fish, there is also the well-known BogaGrip, which is a sturdy, steel-handled clamp that holds fast to a fish's lower jaw and immobilizes the creature until the hook has been extracted. Both the Ketchum Release and the BogaGrip—which also boasts a built-in weighing scale—come in a variety of sizes.

Finally, don't assume that a bleeding fish is necessarily going to die. Fish blood coagulates in water, not air; there is a good chance that a fish that bleeds as you hold it above the water will soon stop bleeding once it's back where it belongs.

Fish Other than Trout

Trout are fairly delicate and require some of the most careful handling in the catch-and-release fishing world. Bass—black, as well as striped—are tougher, require less babying, and, in fact, may safely be handled by being firmly gripped on the lower jaw with a thumb and forefinger, or with a BogaGrip, as the hook is being removed. When you do this, however, make sure you either support the fish's weight or hold it so that it dangles vertically with its tail pointing down; holding it by its lower lip alone with its body parallel to the horizon puts far too much strain on its jaw and can cause a crippling injury.

Members of the pike family, on the other hand—muskellunge, large pickerel, and pike themselves—should never be held vertically, as this places too much stress on their internal organs. Keep them parallel to the water while handling them, preferably right in the water, and, of course, keep your fingers away from that toothy mouth.

Although in almost every case, an ethical angler would never release a fish by throwing it, some saltwater fish recover most quickly when held by the tail and dropped headfirst back into the water. False albacore and other tunas are one such group of gamefish: Knowledgeable tuna guides insist that this drop-release sends a charge of oxygen through the gills, thereby jump-starting the fish following a taxing fight.

Snook and a few other saltwater species can be temporarily immobilized for hook removal by gently gripping them in the middle and turning them on their sides, with the head and tail flopping down from either side of the angler's hand. This "Vulcan death grip," as some Florida anglers call it, has the same narcotic effect on these fish that being turned on its back has on a trout. However, turning snook or most other saltwater fish belly up also works to calm them down.

People who fish in tropical salt waters need to take an extra precaution against a problem that most freshwater anglers never experience: lurking predators. Sharks and barracudas will grab a tired bonefish or other sport fish that has recently been released, and anglers need to be on the lookout for them—both to protect the fish, and to protect their own hands when they have them in the water.

To Net, or Not to Net

In many cases, a fish can be caught and released without the use of a net. Smaller fish can usually be overpowered and brought to the angler's hand while still relatively fresh and full of energy, and then gently shaken from the hook. Larger fish often can be guided into the shallows, cornered, and then set free with a minimum-touch release.

However, when the current is strong and the fish is of any size at all, it can often be difficult to get your fingers or forceps on the fly without first using a net to immobilize the fish. Trying a netless release under these circumstances can result in a lot of extra dancing around on the part of both the angler and the struggling fish—arguably a healthy thing for the angler, but much less so for the fish.

If you have a net, you can always choose not to use it. If you don't have one, you may wish you did when you are trying to get your hands on a fish that you would have released five minutes ago if only you could have gotten it to hold still.

The safest nets are made of rubber—it doesn't press into the fish's flesh—or soft nylon mesh. Nets made of any stringlike material that can "bite" into a fish or rub the protective slime from its skin are best avoided.

The most efficient way of using a net is to hold it below the surface of the water with the front of its frame tipped slightly toward the fish. Calmly guide the fish headfirst over the rim before tipping the net back toward you and lifting. Avoid chasing the fish with the net, as this is likely only to prolong the fight and further exhaust the fish—and may also give it an additional opportunity to escape.

Releasing a Deeply Hooked Fish

Occasionally, no matter how skillful you are with a pair of forceps, you realize that you won't be able to remove a fly without causing a lot of trauma to the fish. One signal that it might be better to give up on getting the hook out is bleeding at the point of penetration: Further bleeding, possibly resulting in the eventual death of the fish, is likely if you continue.

Often, it is better just to cut the tippet and let the fish keep the fly. Studies have shown that the hook will rust within a few weeks, leaving the fish almost as good as new—which is a far better outcome than having it die from blood loss and shock following release.

When sacrificing a fly in order to save the fish, it is best to clip the tippet as close to the hook eye as you can get in order to avoid further inconveniencing the fish with a tag end of monofilament that wags around in its mouth for a number of days or weeks.

When Is It Ethical To Keep Fish—And How Should We Kill Them?

As mentioned earlier in this book, catch-and-release is a management tool, not a religion. Also mentioned was that it is a good thing most fly fishers don't kill anywhere near their legal limits of trout as well as other gamefish, as the limits on many waters are far too generous.

That said, however, it is probably good to kill and eat an occasional fish; not only does a fish meal reconnect us with the roots of our sport, but it also provides us with literal food for thought on the subject of catch-and-release. From time to time, any human practice, habit, or ritual that has become automatic needs to be reexamined before being either reaffirmed or rejected, and our rote release of every fish we catch is no different. In addition, on some waters, and for various reasons, fisheries managers actually prefer that anglers keep a few fish. There is no reason not to oblige them.

However, on most waters where fish reproduce naturally, and especially where they are native, anglers should be aware that when they kill a fairly large and healthy fish—one of breeding age and size—not only are they also killing part of next year's cohort of new fish, but they are depriving the stream, river, or lake of the potential, and potentially eternal, genetic contribution from a fish that has proven its superiority and its fitness to reproduce by having managed to thrive as well as survive. Generally speaking, it is probably better to take a few smaller fish for a meal; not only has nature invested nowhere near as much by way of resources in a small fish, but that small fish's fitness for long-term survival and reproduction is still an unanswered question.

Finally, when we've decided to keep a fish, it is important to continue treating it with respect. It is, after all, a living thing that is about to give up its life for us.

Dropping a live fish into the bottom of a basket or a bag, or threading it through the gill and mouth with a forked tree branch the way my father taught me to do with brook trout, is neither respectful nor humane, in my opinion. As it suffocates in the air, the fish struggles and appears to suffer, and that apparent suffering leaves a blemish on the conscience of the angler—at least, on *this* angler's conscience it does.

Much preferred is a few sharp and decisive blows to the base of the head—as many as are necessary to do the job. The old-timers used to carry a miniature baseball bat called a "priest" just for this purpose. But any appropriately shaped hard object that has sufficient heft will do.

Also acceptable is a quick snap of the fish's spine, if you are able to do this competently. And many people, especially saltwater anglers, like to "bleed" their fish, which not only kills them fairly quickly, but preserves the quality of the meat.

A cooler with some ice in it will also help you do justice to the sacrifice your fish has made.

When you kill a trout, you will soon see its vivid colors begin to fade. Since childhood, each time I've made this observation, it has served as a profound life lesson that carries far beyond fish and fishing.

What to Do If You Unintentionally Kill Or Mortally Injure a Fish On "Catch-and-Release-Only" Water

It does not happen often with barbless, catch-and-release fly fishing, but it does happen: Despite the angler's best efforts, the fish either dies in his or her hands, or because of uncontrollable bleeding or an inability to remain upright, the fish shows us that a live release will not be successful.

If this happens to you, and the regulations on the water you are fishing allow you to keep a fish of the size you have inadvertently killed, then you should keep it. Take it home, prepare it with a recipe that does it honor, and eat it as a sort of sacrament.

On catch-and-release-only water, however, don't even let the idea of keeping that fish cross your mind. While a game warden might believe your story and secretly sympathize with your concern about not "wasting" a fish, he or she will likely cite you for a fishing violation nonetheless. The warden has no choice: To accept "it was dead" or "it would have died anyway" as an excuse would potentially open a loophole big enough for innumerable poachers to drive their pickup trucks through.

Nor is a fish carcass that is returned to nature a "waste" in any sense. It will provide sustenance for creatures large and small throughout the riparian food web—everything from birds to invertebrates—and eventually return to the river in something of its "original" form in the bodies of new, young fish.

I don't recommend tossing an inadvertently harvested fish into the weeds or the woods. Certainly, the ecosystem will make use of it there, but at least for a time it will attract flies, and from a human standpoint if not a natural one, that seems less than fully respectful. In addition, leaving a fish on land is probably a technical violation of your C&R law's inflexible injunction to "release all fish."

By "releasing" it back into the water, however, you are more closely fulfilling the letter of your legal obligation. You can let nature take over from there.

5

Waters, Woods, and Mountains

Also you shall help yourself to nourish the game in all that you may, and to destroy all such things as are devourers of it.

Fly fishing is such an absorbing pastime that anglers often concentrate, to the exclusion of almost everything else, on the piece of water they happen to be standing in or floating on. But waters do not exist separately from the land and sky that surrounds them; every river, stream, lake, pond, and tidal flat is one component of a much larger system of natural features, processes, and living things. The water in the river comes from rain and snow that fall on mountains and woodlands; the forests through which the river winds shade and cool the water so that the fish can live. Any unhealthy element in the air or on the land will find its way into the water.

To care for the forests, shorelines, and air is also to care for the fish. It is in the best interest of anglers not only to advocate for the health of the waters we fish, but also for the integrity of the larger natural system that connects to and sustains those waters.

Native Fish

Montana's Smith River, a tributary of the Missouri, flows through a spectacular limestone-walled canyon. Anglers often spend several days floating and camping on the Smith as they fish for rainbow trout as well as for healthy browns that lurk like trolls in little limestone caves just below the waterline. Occasionally, someone will catch a cutthroat—and whitefish, which almost nobody tries to catch, are plentiful.

A Smith River guide once told me a story about the time he rowed a movie star down the river in a rubber raft. Like many Western anglers, the actor, whose work included the lead in one or two movies with a strong environmental theme as well as a number of roles as a professional athlete, did not care for whitefish. Every time he caught one, he would wind up and pitch it like a fastball against the wall of the Smith River canyon. I have always imagined that the smack of a decent-size whitey hitting the rock made a bit of an echo in the canyon, as did the splash as the shattered fish reentered the river.

In deference to his famous client, the guide, Brian, held his tongue for a time. Finally, however, he could stand it no longer.

"Mr. _____," Brian said. "Please stop killing the whitefish. They're just about the only native fish we have left in this river."

Part of caring for an ecosystem involves determining what belongs there and what does not. This is not an easy task in a time when our waters and landscapes have become overrun with plant and animal species that have been introduced by humans, either intentionally or inadvertently, from far-off lands.

This alien invasion is far deeper and more widespread than most of us suspect. Think, for instance, of all the plants we grow that come from somewhere else—many of which have gone wild and spread through our landscapes like green wildfire.

Chances are, even the worms in your garden belong to species that originated in Europe or Asia. For one specific example, the big annelid we fishermen refer to as the "nightcrawler" is actually a European, and not an American species at all. Also European in origin is one of North America's most important pollinators: the honeybee.

Our lakes and rivers, likewise, are full of plants and animals that evolved elsewhere.

Clearly, it is unrealistic to expect that we'll ever be able to turn back the clock to a time when everything around us—except for *us* of course—was native to our continent. Our job, then, as ethical but practical caretakers of the outdoors, is to do two things regarding our native and nonnative species:

- Determine which of the nonnatives are doing harm to our ecosystems and either eliminate or diminish them, and,

- Do what we can to protect our native species, many of which are harmed by non-natives that either compete with them or prey on them.

Freshwater native gamefish are in dire straits throughout most of their North American ranges. In the East, native brook trout have been forced to retreat to tiny headwater streams in the face of human activity that has raised water temperatures and covered spawning beds with silt by stripping trees from the watersheds. Although the brown trout, a European native that is less sensitive to water conditions, has taken the brookie's place in many waters, its population usually must be artificially replenished with hatchery stock.

Meanwhile, the Atlantic salmon, all but extirpated in the United States by dams that block it from its spawning water, hangs on—but barely—in just a handful of Maine rivers.

In the Pacific Northwest and on the West Coast of Canada, sea-run rainbow trout (steelhead) and Pacific salmon have been reduced to a small fraction of their former populations by dams, unsustainable commercial fishing, and rising water temperatures.

Many anglers are surprised to learn that the rainbow trout—a fish of the West Coast and the Asian Far East—is not native to America's Rocky Mountain West, where it is now widespread and plentiful. Most of the salmonid species that *did* evolve in the Rockies—grayling, bull trout, and a kaleidoscope of cutthroat trout subspecies—are in deep trouble. Their problems result mainly from damming and other human manipulations of Western rivers, as well as from competition from such introduced species as rainbow trout and brown trout.

The pervasiveness of the rainbow trout is a particular problem for cutthroats, as the two species will readily interbreed to produce a hybrid called a "cuttbow." Because rainbows breed faster and are more numerous, in many waters the cutthroat gene pool has been getting increasingly diluted.

In most cases across the country, environmental conditions have changed so greatly that it is not realistic to think that we could ever bring about complete restoration of native fishes. We can, however, join together and work to protect the last sanctuaries of our aboriginal natives. This protection generally involves trying to spare watersheds that are home to natives from severe cutting and overdevelopment, as well as by taking measures to prevent the introduction of nonnative species that might either eat or outcompete the natives. Sometimes, defending the natives involves advocating for the removal of a dam that changes water temperatures, destroys the character of a river, and blocks access to spawning habitat.

Occasionally, however, a rare opportunity arises to right an old wrong. Conservation-minded fisheries managers will gain access to an isolated stream, pond, or stretch of river that, if cleared of nonnative fish, would make an ideal habitat in which to restore a native species that otherwise would be doomed to dwindle away in a few shrinking tag ends of water that it must share with aggressive interlopers. Perhaps the most celebrated success story to date is that of Colorado's greenback cutthroat trout subspecies, which in the 1970s was given a new lease on life through a program of aggressive management. Just a few years after the beleaguered and nearly extinct greenback was transplanted into a number of Colorado streams that either were naturally fishless, or that had been cleared of nonnative fish through chemical means, the subspecies was able to be downlisted under the U.S. Endangered Species Act from an "endangered" species to being merely a "threatened" one.

A more recent success was that of New Mexico's Gila trout, a distant cousin of the rainbow trout, which by the late 1990s was doing fairly well in a number of streams from which the alien trout species had been removed via chemical treatments and electrofishing. The Gila trout's close relative, the Apache trout, also benefited from similar assistance in Arizona.

We should seize these opportunities when they come along, and support those who are doing the work *even when the nonnatives being removed are gamefish that we like to catch.* And I would argue that this is equally important even if the species to be restored is not one that we particularly like to fish for, because each time we do so, we will be saving an irreplaceable masterpiece of nature as well as an important part of our natural heritage.

Our experiences in the outdoors are always enriched when we know that our surroundings are not entirely artificial: That native birds and animals roam the land around us, and that native fishes still swim in some of our streams.

And when the fish being given a new lease on life *does* happen to belong to a gamefish species, our sacrifice of some brown or rainbow trout water will be repaid many times over by our having preserved for ourselves and for future generations a fishing experience that in the coming decades will be increasingly hard to come by—the possibility of fishing for a native species in the waters where it evolved.

We anglers fish in order to interact with nature, and fishing does not get any more natural than that.

Wild Trout

We can't always have native trout, much as we might prefer them. But on many of our waters, we can still have *wild* trout—non-native fish that nonetheless have adapted well and are able to maintain their own populations.

Anyone who has caught wild trout recognizes their superiority to prefabricated hatchery fish: Not only are they strong, healthy, and colorful, but they radiate a life energy—a glow of vigor and spirit—that is almost entirely missing from the dull products of the fish culturist's concrete raceways.

Like any livestock, trout from hatcheries are bred to survive and grow amid the stresses and crowding of factory farm confinement. Once exposed to the entirely different stresses of a natural environment, relatively few survive even long enough to feel the bite of an angler's hook. Wild nonnatives, on the other hand, while they might not have evolved in the water where the angler encounters them, have demonstrated their worthiness to live there by passing, and continuing to pass, a gauntlet of daunting survival tests that includes evading a legion of hungry predators, competing with others of their kind for feeding lies and food, withstanding the unrelenting push of current, and surviving the deprivations and hardships of an icy winter or two. It is no wonder that national and local angler's groups alike almost universally advocate for wild-trout fisheries wherever they may be found.

Wild-trout advocacy mostly involves taking commonsense steps to avoid human interference with reproduction and growth. The elimination of stocking, or at least its curtailment, is one of the most important, because research has shown that stocked trout tend to have a severely disruptive effect on the wild population. One of angling literature's most poignant—and rueful—accounts of just how rapidly hatchery fish can degrade or even destroy a native fishery is that of the English author Harry Plunket-Greene, in *Where The Bright Waters Meet*, his 1924 book about the Bourne, a small tributary of the River Test. At several points in this moving combination of love letter and eulogy to the Bourne, Plunket-Greene describes the chalk-stream's robust, beautiful, and elegantly adapted native brown trout prior to any stocking:

> "The Bourne trout was a perfect specimen . . . short and deep, with a diminutive head and a tremendous shoulder, bright silver mostly, some yellow-gold, with strongly marked spots, and looked a picture either in

the water or on the bank. He fought like a tiger, and he was, above all, a gentleman.

. . . I should like to emphasize that these . . . were all 'wild' fish who had never tasted horse-flesh in their lives, had probably been spawned a few yards from the place where they were caught, and had grown to maturity in that upper mile of water. They were yeoman stock (no wonder they looked thoroughbred.) Their fathers and mothers had made their living for generations on the same weed and gravel farms.

. . . I have seen two-pounders and three-pounders swimming about in the shallows with their back fins out of the water and fairly bursting with health and defiance and high spirits. It was a wonder to us all how they managed it, for no one did a thing for them; nature did it all herself."

Then, in 1905, Harry and some of his friends made the unfortunate decision to assist nature in her job of fish production by stocking several hundred two-year-old hatchery brown trout along with as many as 2,000 yearling fish into a stream that was already maintaining a perfect balance between the trout and the insects they fed upon, after which the author observes, reflects upon, and records the horrifying results of their tampering:

"As everyone knows, the chalk-stream trout, when he grows to a size of authority, takes up his quarters in a comfortable place with his tail against a stone, or a pile, or a patch of weeds, where the current will bring him down the food without any bother on his part. This beat he will hold against all comers and here he will stay at his ease, sucking in whatever the gods send him, without ever moving away, except to chase off interlopers or make an occasional tailing excursion into the weeds after shrimp, and returning in each case to his old stand to take up position again. If the food comes along in plenty, he gets strong and fat; if it does not, he starves, for he will not go to look for it.

. . . One could see the game being played under one's eyes—the old fish in position slowly wagging his tail and waiting for the millennium, and the little two-year olds darting about in front of him and snapping up everything eatable before it could reach him. One saw him early in the season chasing them away furiously and dropping back to his stand; and then, as time went on and he grew weaker, his rushes became fewer and shorter, till at last he just lay there enervated, inert, blue and blind, and one lifted him out in mercy in the landing-net and put an end to him."

The large, spawning-age natives vanished over the course of a season, and road paving and other human-generated environmental changes occurring at around the same time or soon thereafter made it impossible for Plunket-Greene and his associates to reverse the catastrophic effects of their hideous error. Decades later, the author was still waking up in the middle of the night, haunted by regret. His chapter on "The Tragedy of the Bourne" ends with these words:

"That was thirty years ago. Think of it! Thirty years to emerge from the swoon of starvation to which we sent [the river]. And she can never be the same again; for up above the viaduct the trees and the flowers and the snipe and the wild bees are gone and the great silver trout with them, and the place thereof knoweth them no more."

Low bag limits or, preferably, catch-and-release-only regulations, are also necessary to conserve wild fish of breeding age. In rivers where a wild-trout population exists below a dam, the dam must be operated in such a way that water levels and temperatures remain within a range that allows for successful spawning.

Additionally, there are measures that individual anglers can take to improve their wild-trout fishery. One is to be aware of areas in a river or stream where fish have spawned, and to avoid trampling them. Another is to refrain from fishing for trout that are occupied with spawning, even when the law allows us to.

Diseases and Pests

Over the past several decades, as anglers have traveled across the continent, even across the globe, in pursuit of their sport, a number of unwelcome organisms have hitched rides with them on their fishing boats and on their footwear. For just a couple of examples, in the Rocky Mountain West, the microorganism that causes deadly whirling disease, an illness that deforms and kills young trout, has hopscotched from river to river and watershed to watershed on the boots and waders of fishermen. Meanwhile, on the other side of the world in New Zealand, the slimy algae called "didymo" are smothering life at the bottoms of that country's clear trout streams. Because didymo—or "rock snot"—is native to North America, the best guess as to how it arrived Down Under is that it traveled on the fishing gear of visiting American anglers.

Numerous invasive water plants—Eurasian milfoil and hydrilla, among others—are spreading through lakes and ponds across America, hitchhiking their way on the hulls and trailers of fishing boats. Once these plants get into a piece of water, they spread rapidly, outcompeting and crowding out native water plants as they form dense mats that reduce aquatic oxygen levels and smother fish habitat. They are invariably difficult to remove.

The very least we anglers can do is to make sure we are not unwittingly bringing about the introduction of organisms that will kill our fish and choke our waters. The regulation books and websites of most state fish and wildlife agencies contain information on the pests and invasives of most concern in their regions, as well as the steps that individuals should take to avoid abetting them.

It is in the interest of our sport to keep ourselves educated about these threats, and to take the necessary steps to avoid them.

Getting the Lead Out

Lead is a toxic element that for many generations anglers have used to make weights for fishing; fly fishermen have long purchased it in the form of split-shot to crimp onto their leaders. When lost on the bottom of a river, stream, or lake, lead split-shot lasts forever, and while it does not seem to have a direct effect on the health of fish, it unquestionably damages and degrades the ecosystem on which wild trout depend.

Shot-size pieces of lead are often consumed by water birds, which, like all birds, eat small stones for use in their digestive process. Once eaten, the lead can have a variety of neurotoxic effects, and can also affect reproduction. Predators, such as eagles and other birds of prey, as well as scavengers of all types and sizes, collect high concentrations of lead in their bodies from consuming waterfowl that have eaten the stuff. In this way, lead spreads through the entire riparian food chain.

People who partake of wild waterfowl can also accumulate their share of lead. Some states have taken the wise step of outlawing the use of lead in fishing. Others have lagged behind.

In any case, there is no longer any reason or any excuse for using lead. The sport-fishing industry now produces an array of nontoxic alternatives, from conventional sinkers and split-shot made of steel and other safe metals, to moldable pastes that help a fishing line sink.

Not only should anglers use lead-free weights, but they should spread the word to the less well-informed. Loaning someone else—whether a fly angler or a spin fisherman—some of your nontoxic material, as well as talking to them about the need for it, is a good and necessary way to help your river.

Carry In, Carry Out

All but the shortest strands of monofilament discarded in the woods or on the bank of a steam can entangle birds and other wildlife.

I have seen birds hopelessly wrapped in it after gathering it for use as nesting material.

In addition, the discovery of monofilament woven into the bankside bushes—or the sight of any other streamside litter, for that matter—detracts significantly from the fishing experience.

It is a good idea to either carry a small trash bag with you when you go fishing, or to reserve a fairly large pocket of your fishing vest for the storage of monofilament tag ends, leader packages, sandwich wrappers, beverage containers, and other trash—your own, as well as those left by anglers who have not yet learned a proper respect for the outdoors.

Natural vs. Artificial Fly-Tying Materials

We have already discussed fly hooks, and how they have been shown to break down in the water over the course of weeks and months. So too will natural fly-tying materials—feathers, furs, and cotton threads—fairly quickly disintegrate in an underwater environment. However, many contemporary flies are tied with artificial materials that do not readily break down, and which therefore remain in the environment for a long time after they have been lost by the angler.

Flies that do not biodegrade could be justifiably viewed as a form of micro-litter. And while it seems likely that manmade tying materials will be with us from now on, fly tiers probably should at least give some consideration to the natural alternatives when sitting down at the vise.

Take an Active Role in Conservation

One angler working by her or himself can save significant numbers of wild fish, make a favorite river a little cleaner than it otherwise would have been, and influence many other anglers and non-anglers alike to give more thought to their relationship with the outdoors. But when anglers band together, their power to make change that is beneficial to fish and wildlife increases exponentially. In all parts of the country, not only have anglers' groups affected regulations, stocking regimes, and other sport-fishing policies at the state level, but they have even caused dams to be removed from rivers.

A significant part of taking an active role involves understanding the specific threats to fishing waters in our own regions, as well as on the continent as a whole. Gone are the days we could focus our attention on just a handful of problems: dams, development, deforestation in watersheds, road building, and "water pollution," by which we usually meant industrial waste and untreated or poorly treated sewage that degrades the overall quality of our water. Although all of these factors still play, and will continue to play, a major role in making our waters less habitable to fish, the threats, like everything else in this century, are more complex and varied. Additional challenges include:

As I am writing these chapters, oil is spewing into the Gulf of Mexico from the catastrophic blow-out of the Deepwater Horizon sea-floor oil well there. This is America's largest environmental disaster to date, and it threatens all fish, birds, and other wildlife in the Gulf, and perhaps far beyond. For one worrisome example, bluefin tuna, already pushed toward population collapse by commercial overharvesting, are currently attempting to spawn in the Gulf as the well flows unchecked, and it is unknown what effect the oil and the dispersants used to combat it will have on their reproductive success; nor do we know how badly the oil and chemicals will damage the intricate food chain on which larvae and young of bluefins and other fish depend.

British Petroleum, the company that owns the well, and even the U.S. government seem helpless to get this gusher plugged—and even when the flow of oil finally *is* stopped, I believe that it will take years before we know the full extent of the environmental damage.

Other types of industrial extraction—of hydrocarbons as well as other resources—either are harming, or have the potential to harm, terrestrial watersheds and the fish that inhabit them. Underground water supplies as well as rivers and streams can be contaminated by hydraulic fracturing, or "hydrofracking," a process by which water and chemicals are pumped into the earth at high pressure in order to force natural gas to the surface. These fluids can then seep into the aquifer. Much hydrofracking takes place in the Northeast—including in Pennsylvania near the Catskill Mountains, one of the cradles of American fly fishing.

In western Canada, meanwhile, large amounts of toxin-bearing water are also used in the extraction of hydrocarbon deposits known as "tar sands." After usage, this water is then stored in lagoons, from which it has the potential to escape and make its way into previously uncontaminated surface and groundwater.

Throughout the Rockies, arsenic and cyanide find their way into rivers after being used to separate metals—gold and copper—from ore that has been dug from the mountains.

Mountaintop removal—a highly destructive method of coal extraction—continues to destroy trout streams in the Southeastern United States. As the name implies, miners scrape off the tops of Appalachian mountains in order to get to the coal that lies beneath; the mountaintop itself is dumped downslope into the valley below, where not infrequently it fills and smothers a stream.

As mentioned earlier in this chapter, growing numbers of rivers, lakes, and streams across the country face hostile occupation by invasive species of all types, from microorganisms, such as the whirling disease parasite, that are directly killing or crippling rainbow and cutthroat trout in the Rockies, to plants such as hydrilla that are choking the life out of rivers and lakes almost everywhere, to alien fish such as Asian carp, famous for leaping into passing boats, which are currently crowding out native species in the Mississippi River drainage. Also of extreme concern are a number of exotic mollusks, including zebra mussels from Eastern Europe, first detected in the Great Lakes in the 1980s, which are currently blanketing the bottoms of waterways and filtering the nutrients from waters as far south as Tennessee and Arkansas, as well as New Zealand mud snails, a species that is outcompeting native snails and insects and thereby reducing the amount of food available to fish in the Rockies and Great Lakes regions, along with parts of California and the Pacific Northwest.

Invasive species are invariably difficult, if not impossible, to eliminate once they have taken hold in a watershed.

Mechanized fishing for all types of ocean species is threatening marine fish and marine environments everywhere. Often the cause for the decline in a gamefish population is direct, as has happened to bluefin and other tunas as well as striped bass and many other species worldwide because of overharvesting. But sometimes the effect is indirect, such as when commercial harvesters target a forage fish—for example, menhaden, or "bunker" off the East Coast of the U.S.—and end up taking so many of them that populations of predatory fish—bluefish and stripers, in the case of menhaden—are forced to seek other sources of food.

The drawing-down of aquifers and the dewatering of rivers is a particular problem in the mountains of the West and other arid and semiarid environs. Sometimes water is taken for the sake of a thirsty, and growing, human population. At other times, the water is diverted for crop irrigation. Either way, the fish lose feeding and breeding habitat; in addition, less water often spells warmer water temperatures for fish and other creatures that require a cold environment.

A chronic problem in the Northeast is the constant sifting of airborne neurotoxic mercury onto our waters. The mercury is belched into the air by the coal-fired power plants of the Midwest; it is then carried eastward by the prevailing winds; settles out onto our ponds, lakes, and rivers; and begins working its way through the food chain. Fish themselves apparently don't live long enough to be seriously affected. Instead, the toxin works its way up, and fish predators such as loons, bald eagles, and humans end up accumulating unacceptable levels of mercury in their bodies. In fact, the Maine fishing regulations booklet perennially warns against frequent meals of freshwater fish—especially for children, pregnant women, or women of childbearing age, all of whom are currently advised not to eat *any* fish from the state's inland waters other than a monthly bite of brook trout or landlocked salmon, due to the threat of mercury.

With increasing frequency, scientists have been finding that fish in waters near some of our urban areas are being affected by unconventional types of water pollution, including "secondhand" pharmaceuticals. Once excreted from the human body, many drugs such as artificial hormones from birth control pills pass through sewage treatment largely unaltered, and are ending up in the flesh of fish. Hermaphroditic bass—that is, bass with the reproductive organs of both sexes—have been found in the Potomac and other rivers, apparently as a result.

The ongoing, seemingly inevitable global climate change spells not only a rise in water temperatures, along with possibly drier conditions in many places, but it also could make many North American ecosystems much more hospitable to invasive species of all types that prefer a warmer environment.

Nor does the list above comprise a *complete* roster of the challenges faced by twenty-first-century fish and fishermen . . .

Over the past few decades, much of the freshwater conservation work involving such species as trout and salmon has been conducted by Trout Unlimited. The country's preeminent coldwater conservation organization, TU does hands-on work as well as fights legal battles "to conserve, protect, and restore North America's coldwater fisheries and their watersheds."

Since the 1960s, TU National and its many member chapters—there are around four hundred now, from Maine to Alaska—have been tireless and extremely effective advocates for native and wild coldwater fish. Members of the local chapters also share good times even as they are rolling up their sleeves to do river cleanups and run fishing clinics for kids.

Every conservation-minded angler in the U.S. who is not already a member of TU—about 150,000 currently are—should give serious thought to joining. You can find them online—including information on how to find the local chapter nearest you—at www.tu.org.

6

Other Fishermen
and Women

**For when you propose to go on your sports in fishing,
you will not desire greatly many persons with you,
which might hinder in letting you at your game.**

A friend who is somewhat older than I once described for me a ritual that frequently took place back in the days when our streams, and the world at large, were less crowded places. He told me that upon spotting one another, two solitary fly fishers would often take a break from fishing and move toward some midpoint on the stream or riverbank. As they drew within speaking distance, each would take out his or her fly box, pop it open, and hold it out for the other to inspect. Following this informal ceremony, they would spend some time discussing fly choices and various other aspects of the day's fishing as well as angling in general, until finally they shook hands and parted as friends.

These days, such camaraderie is far less common among anglers. Although people are still friendly enough, strangers astream are now as likely to ignore one another as they are to converse or even to wave. And in situations where anglers are plentiful and onstream real estate is not, angry stares and even harsh words are sometimes exchanged.

But it is necessary to keep in mind that other anglers should be our allies, not our competitors; we need one another not only for the conservation battles we must fight, but also to stand with us in promoting the image and interests of our sport to the general public.

Still, there is just no getting around the fact that some waters *are* crowded, and it is only human sometimes to feel less than delighted when we find ourselves in a crowd of fly flingers we have never met before. Following are some general rules of the road and points of etiquette for maintaining peace, if not harmony, on our fishing waters. It is also important to point out here that people who fish using other methods—spin fishers and, yes, even bait fishers—deserve every bit as much courtesy as do our fellow fly anglers.

The Spot Belongs to Whoever Gets There First. No Exceptions.

In fishing, as in so many things, the early bird gets the worm. No angler owns a fishing spot unless he happens to possess a legal deed to that particular section of ground and water. If someone "beats" an angler to a spot that he or she had planned on fishing, then the newcomer needs to find another spot—one that is far enough away that it does not interfere with the man or woman fishing in the original place.

When a stream is narrower than two long casts across, a newcomer taking up a position on the bank opposite the original person may still be guilty of crowding. In addition, an angler taking a streamside break or sitting and studying a piece of water without casting is still fishing that water; no one should try to swoop in and take over.

It is in the best interest of all of us to be good sports about this rule: The next time around, we may be the one occupying the hot spot, and of course, we'll expect everyone else to respect our rights to fish it freely.

It's OK to Ask—But Don't be a Pest

Sometimes a particular pool or other "spot" seems large enough to accommodate more than one angler, provided both anglers are friends, or at least on good terms. Newcomers should feel free to ask the earlier arriver if it's OK to fish nearby. Often the answer will be "Sure." But if it's some version of "no," it's better to move along than to fuel bad feelings.

Give the Other Person Plenty of Room

It used to be that anglers worked hard to fish out of sight of other anglers. This goal is now unachievable in most places, and giving one another as much space as possible is the best we can hope for.

Custom sometimes determines how close to others an angler should position himself on the river. On steelhead and salmon waters, for instance, an angler traditionally works his way down a run, taking a step or two downriver after every cast. An angler who is working a run has a "right" to the entire stretch no matter how long it might be; no one should "low-hole" him by wading in below—although it is usually fine to step in at the top once there's sufficient space between you.

On trout water where there's no particular custom, a new arrival to the river should take a minute to study what the other anglers are doing. If another fisherman is dry-fly fishing and working his way upriver, it would be unmannerly to step into the water above him. Instead, the newcomer should enter downstream, and then either head downriver or work his way upstream, giving the other person plenty of room and fishing the water he has already covered. If the other angler is nymph or streamer fishing, on the other hand, and working his way downriver as he does so, the new arrival should avoid entering the river below him. Heading upstream instead is a good choice, as is waiting until there is a respectable space between the two of you and then fishing along behind the other guy. The amount of space you should allow will depend on how crowded the water is; if a lot of anglers are out, spacing will be necessarily tighter. But if there is no one else about, it is a good idea to wait until the other person has moved out of sight before following in his footsteps.

On rivers where anglers tend to stake out a spot and then stay put, never moving much in either direction, a newcomer usually can't go wrong by taking a position at least two long fly casts away from any other angler: This will prevent any competition for a particular fish, as well as any tangles of terminal tackle. On many crowded rivers, however, ideal spacing between anglers just is not possible; people must fish closer to one another out of necessity. However, at some ill-defined point, "closer" becomes "too close," and hard feelings can arise. Anglers should remain aware of one another's "personal space," which on any trout stream means the minimum area required for a fly fisher to fish comfortably without feeling hindered or harassed. Anglers should develop a good sense of that personal space, respect the personal space of everyone else, and hope that everyone respects theirs. And, if there is any uncertainty, talking to the other angler in a friendly way will probably prevent misunderstandings.

Do Not Cast to Another Person's Water

The fact that you are able to reach a particular fish or fish lie doesn't necessarily mean that you *should* make the cast—not if somebody who arrived on the scene ahead of you is already working that zone. In addition, if a fish you decide to work is part of a pod, casting to or hooking it stands a good chance of spooking all the others feeding close by, thereby ruining the fishing for any angler who got there ahead of you.

Generally speaking, an angler has a claim on all the water he can reach and to all the fish he or she happens to be casting to, as well as to all other fish in the immediate vicinity. If there is any question, it should be asked before it is acted upon.

The larger point of etiquette to keep in mind is that *an angler should always try to avoid doing anything that compromises another angler's chances of hooking a fish.*

Considerate Wading and Walking

Anyone who has been fishing more than once knows that wading too close to fish puts them down. Anglers should take pains to wade far enough from where another person is fishing to avoid spooking any fish within his or her casting range.

Likewise, tromping too close to the riverbank, especially if you are casting a shadow over the water, can ruin a good part of somebody else's fishing day. An angler walking a riverbank who spots another person either wading close to shore or watching the river from the bank is well advised to take an inland detour of ten or more yards in order to avoid affecting the fish.

Anglers in Boats

Anglers in any type of watercraft—drift boats, motorboats, jet boats, canoes, kayaks, kick boats, pontoon boats, and float tubes—should behave in a courteous manner toward wading anglers as well as other people fishing from boats. Generally, this means respecting the rights of anyone who has reached a particular fishing spot ahead of you, as well as following the Golden Rule of not doing anything to spoil someone else's chance at a fish.

Whenever possible, a boat traveling downriver should pass *behind* a wading angler in order to avoid disturbing the water in front of him or her. If passing behind is not possible, then the boat operator should try to pick a route that, at minimum, is beyond the range of a long fly cast from the other person—the farther the better. In cases where neither passing behind nor far beyond is possible, the best course often is to cut directly in front of the angler, passing as close to him as you can in order to avoid disturbing more of the water within his or her casting range than is absolutely necessary. If you can stop your craft a good distance upstream, and then get out and walk it past the angler, so much the better; not only will you minimize the amount of noise you make, but you will eliminate the risk of striking the other person with an oar or a paddle. However, because the angler might not understand that you've got a good reason for coming so close and forcing him to stop casting—and that you're doing it for his benefit—as you come within hearing distance you will need to start explaining your actions. A smile and a friendly voice will be necessary here—and an apology is probably also in order.

Anglers in watercraft also need to avoid fishing the water that rightfully "belongs" to anglers whom they pass as they drift downstream. If a wading angler can reach a piece of water that lies in front of him, then any angler in a passing boat, canoe, or kayak should avoid casting to that water.

Wading anglers, for their part, should realize that people in watercraft have no choice but to continue downstream. If you are fishing in the navigable channel of a river, you should be tolerant of boats and other craft that pass through "your" water.

People in boats are also responsible for the safety of anglers either anchored or wading downriver of them. Wading anglers cannot wade fast enough to avoid being struck by a boat; nor can anchored boats usually pull anchor fast enough to maneuver out of the way. Therefore, anyone downstream always has the right of way, and it is the responsibility of the boat operator to be aware of who and what is occupying the water below, and to take the appropriate precautions.

How to Handle a "Tangle" with Another Angler

Leader tangles happen from time to time. Usually, the person closest to the tangle brings it in and sorts it out. The main exception is when the other angler is a child; then it is the adult who should probably do the untangling. In situations where the person doing the untangling can't get the job done without cutting the other person's leader, he should explain what he's doing beforehand.

If repeated tangles occur, arguing about the problem does little good. The anglers need either to give one another more space, or if that is not possible, shorten up on their casts.

How to Deal with Fly Anglers Less Knowledgeable Than Yourself About Laws, Rules, and Etiquette

If somebody "trespasses against" you or commits some other onstream breach of good behavior, there's an excellent chance he or she is not doing it intentionally. A lot of anglers, even ones who are old enough to know better, have not had the benefit of good example; they are being as good as they can, but they are handicapped by the lack of a clear idea of what "good" really means on a piece of fishing water.

Yelling or snarling at such people usually only makes them defensive and resentful. It's not likely to teach them much—and it provides them with a poor model for settling any other onstream conflicts they may have. ("Oh, so you *are* supposed shout at the other guy . . .)

A friendly comment, in which you come at the issue a little indirectly, is a better way to go, and one that sets the proper example: "You know, I usually like to stand a little farther away from somebody when I'm fishing so I don't spook their fish or tangle their line."

Even better is to take a short break from your fishing in order to have a general conversation with the offending angler. After you make friends with the person, the two of you can then agree on how you'll divide up the water—and that's the time for you to gently point out that, since you got there first . . .

Every time you influence a person to exercise better onstream etiquette, or to be a more ethical angler, you brighten the future of our sport, and also, quite possibly, the future of the resources on which our sport depends.

Be Helpful to Everyone—But Be Scrupulous about Keeping Another Angler's Secrets When You Are Asked to Do So

Of course, an angler doesn't need the pretext of potential conflict in order to influence others. Whenever you see someone struggling with their tackle, or failing to catch fish when conditions for catching them are favorable, the fishing gods have presented you with an opportunity.

Giving a stranger the right fly for the river or the hatch makes you a hero; rerigging a frustrated angler's leader and terminal tackle—and showing them how to do it themselves, provided you do it in a low-key and respectful way—will earn you a lifetime of gratitude. The angler you've helped will look up to you, and will be receptive in the future to your thoughts about conservation, etiquette, and ethics. And, if they're not already a member of a conservation organization such as Trout Unlimited or the Federation of Fly Fishers, there is a good chance they will take your advice to join.

Some experienced anglers also share information about other fishing spots with novices or newcomers to the area whom they meet onstream. I myself have always greatly appreciated it whenever anglers have shared such information with me. It is important, however, to share only your own "secret" spots if you choose to do so, and never anyone else's. If another angler asks you to keep quiet concerning a spot he or she has told you about, then it would be unethical to betray that person's trust.

Those "Other" Anglers

Unless you happen to be on FFO (fly fishing only) water, spin fishers and, where permitted, bait fishers, have as much right to be there as we do. Acting as if they don't belong not only reinforces the not-altogether-unearned image of fly fishers as hopeless snots and snobs, but it is counterproductive from a conservation standpoint.

Those "other" anglers currently outnumber us by at least four to one, and probably by much more. They've also got many of the same interests in conserving fisheries as we do. In politics, the only strength is in numbers, so it is to our advantage to remain on good terms with anglers of all kinds in order to have some allies in the battles we need to fight.

We should treat those other folks with the same courtesy we extend to one another. We should also give them plenty of room to fish—always keeping in mind that we fly anglers, in order to cast properly, require a lot more space than they do, and *this often is a large inconvenience to* them.

Another thing to remember is that, in spite of what they may say, spin and bait fishers often are intimidated by fly fishing: They think it's difficult, and something that one must be some sort of magician to master. This feeling of intimidation often comes disguised as indifference, or even as scorn.

If you show one of them that our way of fishing does not necessarily require a PhD, and especially if you put a rod in their hands and coach them through a few casts, not only are you helping to break down a harmful barrier, but you may be launching the career of another dedicated fly fisher!

How to Behave When Fishing with Guides

If you are lucky enough to be able to afford some guided fishing from time to time . . . yes, your guide is a hired person. However, that doesn't mean that you are the boss.

A fishing guide's main priority among many concerns is the safety of his or her clients. In addition, most guides know far more about fishing than you do—and even if they don't, it's a sure bet they are far more familiar with their particular lake, river, or saltwater flat than you.

If you don't care for a particular fishing guide, you have the option of never fishing with that person again—or even of complaining to the shop owner or outfitter who employs the guide, if he or she does something especially egregious. But, while you are with that person, unless he or she is being openly abusive (see Chapter 9), do what the guide tells you to do.

In addition, don't forget to tip a guide who has done a good job for you. If you're unsure of the customary tip for the area you are fishing, don't be shy about asking a local fly shop manager or fishing lodge owner.

Handling Success

I was once fortunate enough to fish England's storied River Test for a day—a wonderful fishing experience as well as one that, owing to the unfamiliar social situation, was also a bit surreal.

After fishing on my own for half a morning in a landscape that put me in mind of Hobbits, I was retrieved by my "ghillie" and taken to a rustic building to have tea with some of my fellow anglers, all of whom were Brits. As soon as I arrived, I cheerfully briefed one and all about the beautiful, native brown trout and grayling that had fallen for my flies. They all smiled and nodded politely.

I then began interviewing them one by one about how they themselves had done on the river.

"I had a lovely time," responded the first man.

"So, you caught a few, then?"

"It was just a lovely morning."

I then turned to the next man, who answered, "Lovely water."

"Some trout then?"

"Gorgeous morning."

I received similar "lovely day, gorgeous morning, lovely time" responses from everyone I asked. Not a word about a fish.

Later, in private, I asked my host, who was also a Brit, what all this "lovely" business had been about.

"Oh," he said matter-of-factly, "they wouldn't think of *bragging*."

While this all struck me as nothing more than strange at the time—as well as something of a rebuke—I've come to admire the attitude, if not accept it wholeheartedly.

Manners, some famously mannerly person once said, exist to protect the feelings of others. And it *is* true that going on about some huge fish, or huge quantity of fish, you have caught can sometimes make less successful anglers feel oppressed.

I suppose the real caution for an irrepressible American fisherman is to give some consideration to the amount of chest beating he or she does on any particular fishing day. After all, it is not hard to imagine that, one day in the not-too-distant future, we'll be the ones who have come in from a skunking, and it will be some other angler who owns the obnoxious bragging rights, should he choose to exercise them—and how will we feel then?

Know Some First Aid, Just in Case

At some point, you'll need it for yourself, or for someone else. Injuries and health hazards to which anglers are prone range from minor cuts, scratches, scrapes, puncture wounds, and sunburn to broken bones, hypothermia, heat exhaustion, and drowning. Fortunately, most situations you'll encounter in your fishing life will be of the more minor variety—but just in case, you should know the basics of what to do in any situation that might come up on the water or in the woods. There are few worse feelings than that of helplessness during a medical emergency.

Direct pressure with a bandage, bandana, or clean piece of clothing is the right treatment for any bleeding wound, from slight to severe. In fact, pressure and a bandage of some sort to keep the open area clean may be all that's necessary for a minor injury. On the other hand, a wound that is bleeding profusely will of course also require the speediest possible trip to the hospital.

A fishhook that's gone clear through the skin is often most safely removed by clipping off the point with pliers and then backing out the remainder of the hook bend and shank. (This, by the way, is yet another fine reason to fish with barbless hooks.) However, no untrained person should ever try to remove a hook that has pierced someone's eye; the risk of permanent injury and even blindness is too great, and the job needs to be left to a doctor. Broken limbs need to be immobilized prior to the required hospital visit.

Hypothermia is always a risk to anglers even in summertime, and especially when someone has gotten wet. Symptoms include severe shivering, along with loss of coordination and/or confusion and the inability to speak coherently. First-aid treatment involves getting the victim warm again: A change into warm, dry clothes and a hot drink in a warm building is ideal. When no heated structure is available, the interior of a warm car or a campfire will help, as will dry clothes or a sleeping bag and a couple of cups of hot fluids. Alcoholic beverages are *not* recommended.

The symptoms of heat exhaustion include clammy skin, weakness, disorientation, and irritability. The sufferer requires cooling fluids, a rest in the shade with his or her feet elevated, as well as some cool compresses on the neck, chest, and armpits to reduce body temperature. With the proper first aid, a heat exhaustion victim will usually recover fairly quickly—although he may remain somewhat shaky for a while thereafter. *Heat stroke*, on the other hand—in which the victim may exhibit an elevated body temperature, a rapid pulse, hot, *dry* skin, and likely may also be exhibiting strange behavior, or even have fallen into a seizure or become unconscious—is an extremely serious medical emergency that requires rapid cooling to bring the body temperature down, fluids to restore hydration, and quick transport to a hospital for treatment to prevent brain injury or other permanent organ damage.

The best prevention for heat exhaustion and heat stroke is for anglers to stay hydrated while they are fishing or hiking between fishing spots. Anglers should also wear hats and clothing that protect them from the sun, as well as cover any exposed skin with sunscreen in order to avoid sunburn.

Someone who has lost his or her pulse for any reason, including heart attack and drowning, requires CPR (cardiopulmonary resuscitation). I can't even begin to describe this procedure adequately; in fact, you should not attempt CPR unless you have received training. All anglers, and everyone else, for that matter, should take a course in CPR—and then *retake* it every couple of years. You never know when fate might choose you to save a life . . .

A bit beyond the topic of first aid, but still of vital importance, is the proper method for rescuing a drowning person. Always be conscious of your own safety: Try to effect your rescue from onshore or from inside a watercraft if you can, using a rope, a pole, or even a shirt or other article of clothing to pull the victim to safety. A rope, sturdy stick, or other "towing" object is even more important if you must go into the water to save someone; allowing a thrashing, panicking victim to latch onto you while you are trying to help them could put you both in serious danger of drowning together. Of course, if you are not a good swimmer and the victim cannot be saved unless someone goes in after him, you should leave the rescue to someone who does swim well.

Lastly, be aware that in cold water, a swimmer's muscles can stop working in a matter of a minute or less. Under such conditions, trying to swim for almost any distance at all could be a fatal mistake; a rescuer might himself perish before accomplishing his mission, and a person trying to swim to shore from a capsized boat might never arrive. It is much safer, when the water is cold, for a would-be rescuer either to use a boat or to wait for assistance rather than attempting a rescue swim, and for the occupants of a capsized watercraft to cling to their vessel and await help rather than trying to make it to shore on their own.

Please be aware that the above first-aid information is nothing more than a summary; each of us owes it to our fellow anglers, to ourselves, and to our sport to seek further information and education on the subject.

7

The Next Generation
of Anglers

**And all those that do as this rule shall have the blessing
of God and St. Peter.**

As a young spin fisherman with a largely unrequited enthusiasm for trout, I longed to catch fish on a fly rod, and to tie the flies to catch them with. But I had no one to show me what to do, and every book I read on these subjects made them seem even more intimidating, technical—even alchemical—than they had before.

I was an apprentice without a sorcerer.

As a result, my mundane and frustrating spin-fishing career stretched on into my twenties. Finally, a friend's father stuck a fly rod and reel in my hands, briefly explained the train of connections that ran from the reel arbor to the hook eye, and gave me a dry fly that I understood him to say was a "Blue-Wing Doliff." He then sent me out to whip the water. After that, as we fished within sight of one another, he would from time to time look up at me and bark something like "You're bringin' your arm too far back."

Although I barely knew what he meant, at least I was on my way.

Of course, my development as an angler would have gone much further much faster if I'd had a dedicated mentor. But such was not my fate. Instead, as I struggled my way up a steep learning curve largely on my own, I began to take advantage of "minute mentors"—complete strangers I met on various trout streams who would take a few minutes to explain some tactics, give me a fly to use and maybe tell me how to tie it, fuss a bit with my rigging, perhaps even retying a knot or two, suggest a few new fishing spots—or just offer encouragement.

For the most part, these helpful wizards tended to be gray- or white-haired older men who were out fishing by themselves. Many of them wore Flip-Focals clipped to the brims of their hats. In fact, I began to view people matching this description as almost a sure bet, and whenever I spotted one I would speed my way along to the bank to make hopeful conversation. Very few ever failed to sense my need and live up to my expectations—which at the time was a source of astonishment to me. *Why,* I wondered, *would they waste time with the likes of me, when there were fish to be caught?*

After some years had passed, I finally discovered the answer to that question. With the cumulative help of all my many minute mentors, along with some actual fly-tying lessons, I eventually edged into competence as a fly fisherman. And as I did so, I began to realize that, not only was it a warm pleasure to share what I knew with younger anglers, but it was vitally important that I do so.

The future of fish and rivers depended on it.

Now I've become something of a white-haired, Flip-Focaled wizard myself. I've served as onstream minute mentor to innumerable other anglers—and I even remember some of them as well as I am sure they remember me.

Just as important, I have sometimes worked publicly with younger people, teaching them how to tie flies, talking to them about fish and fishing, and trying to channel their natural excitement and enthusiasm for the natural world into an active life outdoors and an appreciation for healthy waters, wildlife, and fish. In this regard, I am just one of thousands of anglers across the country who realize the importance of helping beginning anglers to acquire not just the technical skills of our sport, but also the ethics, the etiquette, the environmental knowledge, and the passion for conservation that will ensure that our sport has a future. It is a critical task, and one each of us should undertake at least in a small way, because without a new generation of ethical anglers and habitat protectors, all the things we care about will fade—and without our hard work to recruit, develop, and encourage them, there will be no new generation of protectors.

Each angler, through his or her own support for conservation and his or her own influence on other anglers through teaching and example, saves a few wild fish and a little bit of fishable water. Each new angler that ethical angler influences does the same. In this way, we and our sport "pay it forward."

How many more developing angler/conservationists could I have influenced by now, if I'd been able to learn fly fishing at a much younger age? The question does not exactly haunt me, but it does sometimes occupy my mind. The answer, I'm sure, is *many*.

In addition, I could have learned, and been well on my way to influencing others, at a *very* young age. You can teach children as young as five to cast a fishable length of line, or to tie a basic fly. And once you do that, simple lessons on such matters as the benefits of catch-and-release and the need for healthy fish habitat will naturally follow.

I think most anglers who teach a child for the first time are surprised at how satisfying it is. Many informal teachers say that teaching kids about fishing is, in its own way, just as rewarding as fishing itself.

Nor, in order to show somebody else, do you have to be an expert at either casting or tying—although each child you work with will view you as *more* than an expert. She'll view you as a wizard, and that slightly ragged Woolly Bugger you help her to tie will light a fire in her mind that will never go out.

A good way to get involved in working with kids is through Trout Unlimited and the Federation of Fly Fishers—although some local divisions of these organizations spend more time working with kids than others. My home TU chapter (Kennebec Valley, Maine), does a great deal with younger anglers, conducting kids' clinics in the spring, teaching tying to youngsters at fishing shows, and conducting a first-rate, week-long Trout Camp on the Kennebec River each summer. In this way, KVTU has created a lot of young anglers and conservationists over the years.

If your chapter is not yet involved in working with the young, it's probably only because no one has yet come forward to lead the effort. Why not step into the breach, set an example, and start lighting fires that will burn forever?

8

The Public at Large

Also, I charge you, that you break no man's hedges in going about your sports: nor open any man's gates but that you shut them again.

The good news is that, as of this writing—summer, 2010—the nonfishing American public, by and large, still seems to view sport fishing as a largely harmless and wholly wholesome pastime. Of course, occasionally an animal rights group will launch a campaign to publicize the alleged cruelties of our sport, or something will pop up in the media about hooked fish "feeling pain." But up to now, such developments have not gained much traction.

That is not to say, however, that the public consensus can never turn against us or that we anglers can ever take the public's good will for granted. As with any good relationship, regular maintenance is required. Whether we're fishing on private land, or on land and waters owned by the (largely non-angling) public, we should, as the "Treatise" advised us 500 years ago, be scrupulous about leaving "hedges" undamaged and closing all the gates. In addition, while the advice in the "Treatise" was entirely literal, here in the more complicated twenty-first century, we anglers need to think metaphorically as well.

One gate that needs to remain firmly sealed is the one that would let in any doubts about our concern for and intentions toward the resources we use. In our contemporary world of instant and constant communication, public opinion about almost anything can be reshaped in a virtual heartbeat. Not only do we need to behave ethically when we're fishing on land and water that does not belong to us—or, at least, to us *alone*—but we need to be aware that almost everything someone else sees us do or hears us say constitutes a public message. If we're smart, as a group we will continue taking pains to ensure that the messages people receive about us are always the right ones.

For instance, it should go without saying that we, as individuals, should not defile the environment with our discarded leader material, wrappers, and other trash. The public has a right to expect no less—and we certainly deserve no special pats on the back for picking up after ourselves.

However, *when we pick up other people's trash*, either on our own, as a habitual part of every fishing trip we take, or as a group, which we do when our TU chapter or other fishing organization conducts a river cleanup, we are sending a strong message that, not only do we care at least as much as anyone about our natural resources, but that we're willing to put our time and effort into protecting them. Along with demonstrating ourselves to be good citizens, we are also showing non-anglers that, without us, the waters and other resources we use would likely be less healthy.

Likewise, when we attend public hearings and identify ourselves as anglers while speaking up in defense of clean air and clean water, and when we appear in public to teach the children of non-anglers how to cast, how to tie a fly, or about the importance of healthy rivers and wildlife habitat, we are at the same time proving ourselves to be a community worth having in the world.

Also important is letting the public know about any public service or pro-environmental actions we may have taken, in case anyone has managed to miss something good we've accomplished or are about to accomplish. Of course, self-promotion—even the promotion of a worthy group to which we belong—is difficult for many practitioners of our always quiet and often solitary sport. But in almost every fishing club or chapter, there is at least one angler who has had experience dealing with the media, or who even has a gift for this sort of communication. Find that person and put him or her to work; almost any bribe you have to use will be well worth the cost!

Finally . . . I don't really know if fish feel pain or fear. In some sense, they probably do, and in fact, some recent studies suggest as much.

What I *do* know, however, and what I've told the few non-anglers who have brought the subject up, is that there would be far fewer fish in many of America's fresh waters without anglers to stick up for them. All across the continent, anglers and other outdoorspeople have fought battles against an array of commercial interests intent on stripping forests from riverbanks, plundering watersheds for their mineral deposits, dumping poisonous wastes into rivers, and sucking the water from the rivers themselves in order to irrigate crops in semiarid landscapes. Anglers have sometimes even gotten dams pulled from rivers in order to allow anadromous fish to return to their ancestral spawning grounds—in some cases, for the first time in nearly two hundred years. Anglers have also been at the forefront of almost every fight to protect or restore habitat for dwindling native fish species.

Without us, some of these fights either would not take place, or they would take place without the vigor and passion that we lend to them.

It is possible, perhaps even likely, that at some future time American anglers and non-anglers will undertake a serious and continent-wide debate over whether it is morally justifiable for people to catch fish, and especially to practice catch-and-release, purely for sport. In fact, as many anglers will have noticed, such a debate already takes place on a small and intermittent scale here in the U.S., and on a somewhat larger and more regular one in Europe, where the animal rights movement has a larger influence on public policy—one of their signal accomplishments has been the 2005 ban on fox hunting in Britain—and where intentional catch-and-release fishing has already been prohibited in one nation (Switzerland, in 2009).

Though it strikes most fly anglers as bizarre, many animal rights advocates—along with plenty of people who don't subscribe to the rest of the animal rights philosophy or agenda—find catching and releasing a fish to be *more,* rather than *less,* morally objectionable than hooking and cooking that same fish. According to their argument, the fish killer is merely trying to feed himself or his family, which to them is understandable, if not excusable, while the C&R angler is tormenting a living creature for his own amusement, which they view as indefensible.

But when that more serious debate gets underway, it will probably take place in the context of a broader animal welfare discussion in which we as a people try to work out our evolving cultural attitudes toward a host of animal-related activities, including hunting, meat eating, industrial-scale livestock raising, ecotourism—even zoos and the exploitation of animals as entertainers and pets.

We're not quite there yet. When we are, we'll need to realize that those who have moral qualms about what we do may have a point—perhaps not one that is strong enough to base decisions on, but a point nonetheless. We'll have to discuss it intelligently and respectfully—among ourselves as well as with non-anglers.

In fact, not only is the issue worth thinking about, but individual anglers *should* think about it, even if they don't come up with any definitive or even particularly satisfactory answers.

For now, however, and for me, at least, one of the deeply valuable things about fishing is that it combines recreation and exercise in the outdoors with an intimate connection to the natural world in a way that would be impossible to replace. In fact, there is absolutely nothing more effective than fishing for peeling a child away from her computer and getting her out into nature in a meaningful and life-changing way.

In addition, and at this point in the twenty-first century, the most important factor affecting the welfare of fish is the protection of their habitat. *The human action that matters most to fish—species and populations of fish, rather than isolated individuals—is the fight to preserve the health of oceans and watersheds.*

In this fight, anglers are irreplaceable. And without angling itself, not only would fewer anglers—*former* anglers—have a reason to care as much about the problems of our waters, but even those of us who continued to care would be on much less intimate terms with rivers, streams, lakes, and seas; we would not be as aware of what the problems even were, or how environmental conditions might be changing.

Anglers are people who keep their fingers on the pulse of living waters. Not only are we attentive to the health of aquatic environments in a way that other groups are not, but we also care with a passion that others do not share. In the face of an environmental threat, we are invariably the first to rise in defense of gamefish and their habitat. And that, along with the fact that we enjoy it so much, is about all I say if anybody happens to ask me why I think fishermen should fish.

9

How to Treat Yourself

**Also, you must [use] this aforesaid artful sport . . .
principally for your solace and to promote the health of
your body and especially of your soul.**

When I was editing *Fly Rod & Reel* magazine, I asked a writer to interview news anchorman and avid angler Tom Brokaw just prior to Brokaw's retirement after more than four decades in the broadcast business. Brokaw had not discovered fly fishing until he was in his forties, and he told us that he was looking forward to using his free time to significantly expand his fly-fishing horizons. He spoke about trying his hand at heavier fly rods and tackling more challenging fishing conditions. He talked with enthusiasm about how much more he had to learn.

"You can do this sport for a long time," said Brokaw, who was sixty-one when we interviewed him.

He had it right. In addition to being one of the most enjoyable sports in the world, one of the best things about fly fishing is that you can do it, and continue to do it well, well into old age. For just a couple of examples,

Lefty Kreh and Joan Wulff both remained athletic superstars in the fly-fishing world even when they had gotten well into their seventies. Lefty, in his mid-seventies, was still astonishing and amusing crowds at fly-fishing shows by casting more fly line with the top half of a two-piece fly rod than most anglers half his age could throw with the entire rod.

But there's a catch—and the catch is that, when a fledgling fly fisher of any age is starting out, he or she faces a steep learning curve. In addition, the sport is complex enough that, no matter how long you do it and how proficient you get, you'll always make a few mistakes.

Along with an agreeable rod and a dry, comfortable pair of waders, a bit of preparation and a self-deprecating sense of humor are two of the most important tools an angler can possess.

As Anglers, We All Owe It to Ourselves to:

Learn, and Relearn, the Basics Well Enough Not to Get Overwhelmed by Frustration When We Are on the Water

A fly cast involves about the same level of technical challenge as a golf swing. And yet, while golfers cheerfully spend tens of millions every year on lessons, tune-ups, and tips from "pros," many, if not most, fly anglers feel that it is somehow shameful to seek instruction; we seem to believe that, as casters, we are either "good," or "not good," and that asking for help is a tacit admission that we fall irredeemably into the second category. The result, for an angler facing a challenging fishing situation, is often frustration and—in the angler's mind, anyway—failure.

The fact is, even the best casters benefit greatly from being observed and advised by another caster who is at least as good, if not better—so who are the rest of us to think we can do it all on our own?

Beyond technical improvement, an additional advantage to getting some advice is that a knowledgeable casting instructor will spot bad habits that are likely to result in painful shoulder and elbow injuries. I'm fairly certain that, without the counsel of many instructors and fishing guides, I would have long ago suffered a rotator cuff injury.

The Federation of Fly Fishers specializes in the teaching of casting; you can contact them to see if they have a certified instructor near you. Instruction is also available at the many fly-fishing schools around the country, and at most specialty fly shops as well.

Some schools offer "intermediate" or "advanced" classes—but if those aren't available in your area, you shouldn't feel reluctant to join a general class. If you're already an accomplished caster, the instructor is likely to take special pleasure in helping you improve. In addition, he or she will probably *tell* you you're a good caster—something your fishing friends might never do.

Keep Ourselves in Good Enough Physical Condition to Enjoy the Sport in Comfort and Safety

That doesn't necessarily mean going to the gym several times a week—although if that's what you enjoy doing for exercise, have at it. It stands to reason, however, that if we can't walk two or three miles without feeling exhausted, we're not likely to get much enjoyment out of pounding a riverbank while carrying gear on our back, or wading a brisk current full of slick boulders and other hurdles.

At a minimum, an angler should try to take a few long walks—walks that verge on being hikes—a few times a week. Also, we need to do something for our arms and upper body to keep ourselves in casting shape. Even yard work can suffice, if we do enough of it.

In short, do whatever you feel like doing, as long as you're doing *something*. And, when we're not getting a lot of fishing in, it's also not a bad idea to knock the rust off of our casting arms from time to time. We should practice double-hauling, keeping those loops tight, and throwing reach casts to either side. We'll be much sharper then, when the casting really counts.

Avoid Putting Ourselves in Harm's Way

The risks involved in most fishing situations are relatively minor. If the water isn't dangerously cold, we're not far from the bank, and we know how to swim, the possibility of slipping and getting a little wet often is no big deal. On the other hand, the placid appearance of a piece of angling water can be treacherously deceptive—in a matter of seconds, an underwater ridge of gravel can wash out from beneath our feet, a shallow ledge can suddenly fall away into an unseen drop-off, or the pull of a current can end up being much stronger than it seemed. It is important to know the water we're on, as well as to have a realistic understanding of our own physical limitations. Fish with a buddy if you can; you'll have a safer time, and probably a more enjoyable one.

Under unambiguously challenging conditions, or if we have even the smallest doubts about our ability to extract ourselves from trouble, then a fishing partner to look out for us is a necessity rather than an option. If no fishing partner is available, it would be a good idea to save that particular outing for another time, and switch our sights to one involving fewer risks. There is no fishing experience in the world that is worth the life of an angler.

Forgive Ourselves for Our Mistakes—and Look on Them as Learning Opportunities

I once fished a famous Atlantic salmon river in Canada. It was my first experience at Atlantic salmon fishing—and on my second day, I caught the biggest fish taken on the river during the entire year. At the time, I was under the supervision of a very good guide, but beyond that, it was pretty much an accident.

Two weeks prior to this writing, on the other hand, I was casting to a pod of fourteen-inch brown trout that were rising on the Kennebec River, and I could not get one of them to look at my fly. I was doing something wrong, and while I now think I know what the problem was,

I haven't yet been back to test my theory. In any case, I was happy I did not have an audience that day . . .

Some days, we can't do anything wrong. Other days, we can't do anything right. That's fishing; we need to make peace with it.

Try to figure out what you could have done better, and then try to do it better the next time around. If it works out, celebrate. If there's still work to be done, either practice or fly tying or research or just sitting down and thinking, go ahead and do that work—but at the same time, give yourself credit for having made the effort.

If we are in the habit of beating ourselves up over things—I admit that I often suffer from this tendency—we're not likely to improve. In addition, we will probably just get dispirited, and being dispirited is not in the spirit of fly fishing.

An angler may even occasionally commit an ethical lapse; we all, after all, sometimes act on impulse or do things without thinking. If that happens, I recommend making amends as best you can. Apologize or try to fix what you did wrong, and resolve not to do it again. And, try to be brave enough—here's where that self-deprecating humor comes in—to tell others about it, in order to set an example and to help them avoid making the same mistake.

In this way, something good will have resulted from your error.

Learn to Get Satisfaction From Hooking the Fish—or at Least Attracting Its Attention—Rather Than From Landing It

The psychology of catch-and-release fishing is as of yet not fully evolved. While most of us have become almost reflexive about releasing every fish we catch, we still feel the need for the thrill of possession. We have a strong urge to "own" a fish, at least temporarily, either by netting it, or curling our fingers beneath its belly, or by running a tape measure along its shining flank.

As a result, if we don't tactilely count coup on a hooked fish—if the tippet parts after rubbing on a rock or the hook pulls out during a fight—we tend to feel that the catch has not been completed. We feel unsatisfied in much the same way that anglers of a few decades ago felt unsatisfied if they failed to crack their fish in the head with a rock.

I don't think those feelings are helpful, or even necessary, to our sport, and we'd do best to evolve beyond them. Certainly, there will always be an especially large fish that we'll want to measure; curiosity is incurable, after all. And there will be at least as many that are so beautiful that we'll want to "bring them to hand" in order to take a photograph as a memento. But generally speaking, when we're going to let a fish go anyway, what logical reason is there to handle it?

As mentioned earlier in this book, unless a fish is completely exhausted—an outcome that should be avoided in any case—the best release for the health of the fish is the release that involves the least amount of handling. Near perfection in a release consists of the quick twist of a barbless fly with either fingers or forceps, followed by a smile of appreciation on the part of the angler.

But perhaps *absolute* perfection, from the perspective of what would provide the greatest ongoing satisfaction to anglers as well as assure the well-being of the fish, would be the release that did not involve handling the fish at all.

Maybe it's time for a change in status, a new and high level of respect, for the LDR—the much mocked and maligned long-distance release.

We all experience our share of LDRs. Sometimes some of the cause rests with our technique: We've fought the fish inefficiently and therefore for too long, or we've given it more slack than is advisable for barbless-hook fishing. Often, however, an LDR just happens, usually as the result of a precarious hook-set. Rather than seeing it as some sort of tragedy, we anglers would be happier people if we could bring ourselves to view the long-distance release as not only part of the game, but also as a fitting end to a fine experience.

Insist on Good Service and Respect From Those We Deal With in the Professional Fly-Fishing World

We avid amateurs of the fly-fishing world, regardless of our level of experience, need to respect ourselves as people first, and as anglers second. This means insisting that the professionals in our sport—the people who sell us goods and services—treat us in a courteous and respectful manner.

As a matter of course, most specialty fly shop personnel work hard to make all their clients, regardless of skill level, feel comfortable and appreciated, and they also do their best to demystify the complexities of equipment, strategy, tactics, and local hatches. Rather than filling the air with tales of their own angling exploits, they listen to their customers, provide *solicited* advice in a thorough and friendly manner, and offer solutions to equipment needs that fit within the customer's stated budget. When the visit is over, regardless of how much or how little the client has spent, they send them back out to the water with words of encouragement and an invitation to return.

If that is not the way you are being treated at your fly shop, I recommend finding another one, even if you have to drive a long way to get there. Life is too short, and fly-fishing time too precious, to allow unprofessional professionals to spoil any part of them for you.

Fishing guides, for their part, in addition to knowing how to help you catch fish, should remain professional even as they row that rocky channel between entertaining clients, and at the same time instructing them and keeping them safe. It is the guide's job to be firm at times, especially regarding issues of safety. He or she sometimes needs to "tell you what to do," and you shouldn't feel offended by that.

Surly guide behavior, on the other hand, is inexcusable as well as an unmistakable indication that you should never again waste money or time fishing with that person. Nor has a guide got any business seriously complaining about a client's fishing skills. A guide gets paid the same regardless of how competently his or her anglers are able to fish, and the best guides figure out ways to help clients improve their game—even when those clients *think* they already know it all.

Part of the guide's job also involves being something of an amateur psychologist and "reading" his or her clients. For instance, your guide may read you and your fishing companions and determine that it's OK to joke with you, maybe even tease you a little—and that, in fact, you all might have a more relaxing and enjoyable day if he did so. That's wonderful, provided he's "read" you correctly and the teasing doesn't feel to you like belittlement or bullying. If the guide has indeed misread you, figure out a friendly way to get that message across. I suggest eye contact and smile, followed by something like, "You know, I don't usually fish very well with that kind of pressure."

A good guide will take the hint. On the other hand, if he or she is a true, psychologically damaged bully or belittler—there are very few of these, but they do exist—then you're out of luck, at least for the rest of the time you have to spend in their company. The good news is, you'll never have to fish with that person again—and neither will any of your friends, because all of them will have the benefit of your hard-won experience.

10

The Future of Fly Fishing

. . . you should covet
no more at that time.

With the exception of a few distinguished visionaries, fly fishers of even a half century ago could not have begun to imagine our early twenty-first-century angling environment. The idea that nearly everyone would one day be releasing nearly all the fish they caught would have boggled the minds of most of them—and it would have struck more than a few as a terrible "waste" of a perfectly good fish as well as an angler's time. Nor, in an era when the mass production of almost everything was widely viewed as the ultimate answer, rather than as a source of misgivings and endless and skeptical questions, would most have understood the insistence of enlightened contemporary fly fishers that trout bred and spawned in a stream are far preferable to colorless, finless, poorly suited-for-survival hatchery fish, no matter how numerous or catchable they might be.

They'd be in awe at our equipment, which to them would seem light-years ahead of anything they had to work with: The waterproof yet breathable materials that make up our waders, the nearly "magical" graphite technology that gives us fishing rods so much stronger, lighter, and faster than the bamboo and fiberglass to which they were accustomed, the slick fly lines that shoot effortlessly with only the most cursory of care, and the explosion in the variety of fly-tying materials, including many that allow us to create flies the old-timers might have difficulty even recognizing as such.

The global reach and kaleidoscopic variety of our form of recreation—the idea that anglers in considerable numbers would one day be pursuing many species of gamefish throughout the waters and shrinking wildernesses of the entire earth, from the Rocky Mountain tailwaters and the steelhead streams of Kamchatka to the flooded Amazon forests and the bonefish flats of remote Pacific islands —would have astonished mid-twentieth-century fly fishers, most of whom fished exclusively in their local waters.

Of course, we contemporary fly fishers are really nothing more than the "old-timers" of the future, and it is just as impossible for us to envision a clear picture of where fly fishing will be fifty years from now as it was for black-and-white-television-era anglers to imagine life and sport as we are living them now. We do, however, have the benefit of some strong trends to help us make our educated guesses. Unfortunately, most of these trends suggest a contracting fly-fishing world, rather than an expanding one, as well as almost limitless social and environmental hurdles and complexities. To list just a few:

- Fewer anglers overall, as urban and suburban people continue to lose the connection to nature that almost all Americans once had. And, while this might seem like a good thing to some veterans of crowded trout streams, it spells less social and political power for anglers who, as a group, will need every bit of influence they can get.

- Shrinking access to streams, rivers, and lakes, as waterfront property everywhere continues to be bought, subdivided, developed, and restricted to the exclusive use of owners and other privileged inhabitants. This trend will concentrate the remaining anglers on the remaining open waters, causing crowding as well as increased pressure on fish populations.

- Fewer waters overall that are suitable to trout due to rising water temperatures. The temperature increases will result from a changing climate as well as from the continued removal and development of forest land currently serving to cool streams and rivers.

- Greatly reduced numbers of saltwater gamefish due to the ongoing mechanized harvesting of the world's oceans. Such harvesting targets not only the gamefish themselves, but the baitfish and other food sources they need to sustain their numbers.

- Exotic invasive species of all kinds radically changing aquatic environments the world over. Exotics range from the didymo algae ("rock snot")—originally from North America—now spreading through New Zealand's trout streams, where it covers and smothers river-bottom organisms, to the European whirling disease microorganism currently twisting the spines of rainbow and cutthroat trout in the Rocky Mountain West, to the many species of carp that seem to be almost everywhere, and which efficiently vacuum up food meant for native fish species, to the exotic zebra mussels that filter the nutrients out of the water in the Great Lakes and elsewhere.

- Increasing pressure from an animal rights movement that does not care for fishing, and especially not for catch-and-release fishing.

This all sounds, I am well aware, almost too bleak to bear. But, to quote Ebenezer Scrooge, if "the courses be departed from, the ends will change."

If we collaborate with other anglers as well as with hunters, conservationists, environmentalists, and other groups of people who care about woods, waters, wildlife, and human freedom in the outdoors, we can blunt the worst of the change, as well as bring about some changes for the better. We can, as a generation of anglers, fight to ensure that clean, clear water remains in rivers, lakes, and oceans, and that fish remain in all clean, clear waters. We can also insist that a significant number of those waters remain open for use by the people.

Much of this collaboration will involve participating in politics and governmental processes, and using our collective voice. In fact, the term "outdoor advocate" will necessarily come to constitute an indivisible part of what it means to be a twenty-first-century angler. Therefore, it goes almost without saying that, because of our growing need for cooperation—our growing need for *each other*—ethics, etiquette, education, and tolerance among anglers, as well as between anglers and other outdoor recreationalists, will become more important than it ever has been.

Also, in addition to influencing the way society at large—other people, in other words—does things and thinks about things, we anglers will also likely have to make some adaptations of our own by way of reducing our impact on hard-pressed fishing waters. It has become abundantly clear that catch-and-release angling by itself is no longer anywhere near enough to get the job done. Again, current trends suggest possible modifications:

Heightened Awareness of Temperature in Trout Waters

Elsewhere in this book we have discussed the fact that warm water stresses trout, and that catching and attempting to release temperature-stressed trout often kills them, regardless of how careful they might otherwise be handled. In summer, in the Rocky Mountains during recent years, state fish and game officials have temporarily closed some rivers to fishing when the weather has gotten hot enough to threaten the survival of released fish.

In other places, such as the Delaware River drainage in New York and Pennsylvania, conservationists have long recommended that anglers *voluntarily* stop fishing when the water gets too warm. Unfortunately, not all anglers can bring themselves to volunteer.

It is likely that in the coming years, as wild trout and good public trout waters become even more scarce than they are now, anglers themselves will be responsible—either through regulation or owing to a strong, universal ethic as deeply ingrained as C&R itself—for monitoring summertime temperatures in trout streams, and for suspending their own angling after they have risen to a certain level.

Cutoff points of 70 degrees Fahrenheit (21 Celsius) for brown and rainbow trout, and most of the many subspecies of cutthroats, and 65 degrees (18 Celsius) for brook trout, seem reasonable—though it is possible that biologists will tweak these numbers downward in the wake of some yet-to-be-conducted research.

An Unbreakable Habit of Cleanliness

Currently, the disinfecting of boots, waders, watercraft, and other gear before traveling from one river or watershed to another is still treated as an option rather than a firm requirement by anglers. However, in the not-too-distant future, the problem of anglers and their equipment serving as potential vectors for infections and parasites will become too apparent and too acute for any of us to ignore.

We will all become scrupulous about doing whatever is necessary by way of cleaning regimens in order to avoid transferring pests and pathogens among waters. Felt wading boot soles—hard to disinfect completely because of their absorbency—will likely be entirely replaced with rubberlike synthetic materials that are more easily cleaned.

Near-Universal Use of Circle Hooks in Saltwater Angling

Because of their shape, flies tied on saltwater-size circle hooks almost always catch in the corner of a fish's mouth. This affords fish less of a chance of suffering a deep hooking, and therefore a greater chance of benefiting from a swift and minimally traumatic release. In addition, circle hooks have also proven to be effective when used to tie the larger sizes of freshwater flies.

More of a Focus on Freshwater Species Other Than Trout

Trout are among the more sensitive canaries in our environmental coal mine. In fact, one of the reasons we fly anglers care so deeply for them is that, because they require clear, relatively clean, and shaded water in which to live, they serve as a symbol of the vanishing natural wildness that each of us seeks to rediscover every time we go fishing. When we go looking for trout, they draw us to beautiful places.

But there are other freshwater fish—primarily basses and carps, although there are others—which are not so exacting in their survival requirements, that are at least as difficult to catch and that fight just as hard when hooked. They also reproduce quite readily without any help from humans, and are therefore, despite not being native to most waters in which they are found, at least as "natural" as rainbow trout in the Rocky Mountains and on the East Coast, or brown trout anywhere in the world except in and around Europe. These more rugged gamefish species possess the additional virtue of being both common and widespread, and therefore accessible to almost every angler in the country, regardless of where or under what circumstances he or she lives.

In the future, not only will bass, carp, bluegills, crappie, pickerel, pike, mackerel, shad, and other species help to keep the sport of angling alive for us during times when decent trout water is not within our reach, but they will benefit trout and trout water by helping to relieve some of the pressure.

However, to view bass, carp, and other scaly species as merely an acceptable substitute for trout is to sell them short. During the time when the "Treatise" was written, anglers certainly did not look down their noses at any fish that was not a salmonid; in fact, they seemed to appreciate equally all the fishes they were able to catch. If they expressed preference for one fish over another, they generally were judging on the basis of its taste when cooked, not where it lived or what it looked like.

Perhaps, then, as we spend more of our time pursuing fish that are not trout, not only will our sport have come full circle from its beginnings, but as more anglers gain experience with a wider variety of nonsalmonid gamefish, many will undoubtedly begin to appreciate them to the point of specializing in one or more of these species. That specialization, seasoned with a strong dose of passion, will doubtlessly attract equally passionate followers.

Less of a Compulsion Among Anglers to Actually Land a Trout

In spite of a growing recognition among fishermen that being landed and released a number of times takes something out of a fish, many anglers cannot imagine counting a trout as caught without actually "bringing it to hand," as the quaint expression goes. However, it is important to remember that until relatively recently, large numbers of us considered *killing* a fish to be the only satisfactory conclusion to a catch. In other words, attitudes can change—we've changed them in the past—and sometimes, they *need* to change. It could be that one of those times is almost upon us now.

One beneficial adaptation, especially in some of our more heavily pressured fisheries in which trout are caught and released repeatedly, might be to dispense entirely with our habit of equating success and "a good day" with a large number of landed fish, and for catch-and-release anglers to instead begin applying some creative ways of limiting the number of fish they actually fight and handle during any single outing. In order for this shift in attitude to take hold, however, we'd have to begin thinking of fishing as much more of a meaningful and sophisticated play activity—which it is, in any case—and much less of a "hunt" or a "harvest"—which, in any case, it ceased to be as soon as most of us stopped killing our fish.

We mentioned earlier in this book how, when we are fishing flies with barbless hooks, introducing slack to a line will usually allow the fish to do a self-release. Most anglers currently consider the so-called long-distance release (LDR) to be a minor tragedy, even a source of shame, as well as a mistake. But as the culture of angling continues to evolve, the LDR may end up as something that increasing numbers of fly fishers do intentionally with many of the fish they hook, while they reserve the netting and handling of a fish to those times when they want to measure it or take a photo of it.

With intentional LDR fishing, the angler might train him or herself to view the hooking of a fish, rather than the landing of it, as the main reward of angling, just as a pioneering generation of anglers once learned to take its thrill from releasing a fish, rather than from stuffing it into a bag.

The ultimate extensions of this line of thought, however, go far beyond the LDR. There are anglers even today who avoid hooking fish in the first place by using flies that lack hooks. This variation on our sport has been called "hookless fishing" and, more colorfully, "touch-and-go" angling, and its emotional satisfactions reside in fooling the fish, rather than in hooking it, fighting it, or landing it.

According to some proponents of touch-and-go, one big advantage is that trout often keep right on feeding after spitting out a hookless fly, rather than retiring as they usually do after feeling the bite of a hook point. This means that, unless and until you spook a fish with a bad cast and a splashing or dragging fly line, you can "touch" it several times, even trying out different flies and different approaches if you like. No need to move up or downriver in search of another fish, because you still have *this one* to play with, and, meanwhile, the fish itself is barely inconvenienced.

I have no doubt that frequent touch-and-go fishing would teach almost any angler a lot more about trout, and about presenting flies to trout, than he or she already knows. What I am *not* sure of, to be honest, is how fulfilled I would feel as an angler if touch-and-go was the only way in which I interacted with fish. Rather, I currently find that confining myself to dry-fly fishing most of the time is a more satisfying "middle way" between giving trout a desperately needed break on pressured waters and not hooking them at all. Not only is this the way I prefer to fish in any case, but I am also mindful of Lee Wulff's idea—articulated in his 1980 book *Lee Wulff on Flies*—that dry-fly-only fishing gives pressured fish a much-needed "sanctuary" in the deeper water.

But it is possible that touch-and-go will have a place in my angling future. As I've mentioned, I have already gone through far greater shifts in attitude, and perhaps I just need to spend more time thinking about the matter, and also seeking the encouragement of other, better anglers who have already crossed that particular bridge. It may be that the most useful way of looking at touch-and-go fishing is to view 90 percent of all our onstream activity as *prospecting* for fish rather than attempting to catch them. Then, every so often, after we have found an especially large or especially challenging fish, we can allow ourselves to tie on a hooked fly with the hope of bringing that fish "to hand."

In this way, landing a fish would become the climax of an entire half day of fishing rather than the goal of every single cast that an angler uncorks.

Another possibility is that, in the future, anglers will spend significantly more time just sitting and using a good pair of polarizing lenses and perhaps a bit of magnification to observe fish in their natural habitat. Most of us already do this to some extent—though usually our motive is to figure out how best to make a presentation. Perhaps instead, we will eventually learn to derive much of our enjoyment by following the example of birders and wildlifers and devoting at least part of every fishing day to just watching and appreciating fish rather than invariably trying to catch them.

Who can say what else lies downstream of us, through the rapids, and around the next bend? All we know for certain is that we anglers and the sport we love face both challenges and changes. But then, we always have—and, just as in the past, we will need to look to our traditions and our time-tested set of ethics to help us decide how best to face them.

It will continue to be an adventure.

Acknowledgments

As most fly fishermen are probably aware, the late novelist Ernest Hemingway was one of us. Less well known is the fact that Hemingway's literary career was shaped and shepherded by the most gifted, most visionary American book editor of the twentieth century, a man named Maxwell Perkins, who aside from Hemingway also recognized and nurtured such literary giants as F. Scott Fitzgerald and Thomas Wolfe.

The Maxwell Perkins of American fly-fishing books—as both editor and publisher of some of the finest for many decades, as well as an extraordinary angling writer in his own right—is also this book's editor: **Nick Lyons**. To quote Paul Schullery, fly fishing's preeminent historian: "Nobody in the American history of fly fishing has had as positive an influence on the literature of fly fishing as [Nick Lyons] has."

The only two things I have in common with Hemingway are angling and the opportunity to have worked—at least on this one occasion—with a great book editor, and I am extremely grateful for both. I owe Nick a special debt of gratitude not only for his hard work on behalf of *Beyond Catch & Release*, but also for having seen the value of my idea in the first place. Just as we are unlikely ever again to see the likes of Maxwell Perkins, our sport will never know another Nick Lyons; he is a gentleman, an editor, and an angler to be celebrated.

During my years at *Fly Rod & Reel*, I was privileged to edit **Ted Williams**'s "Conservation" column. And, while I was Ted's editor, he, in many ways, was my teacher, and I quickly learned to appreciate him as

America's toughest and most ferocious conservation journalist—as well as a scrupulously accurate one. He is also a friend, and a frighteningly determined angler. I am grateful to Ted for his invaluable help with the environmental and fish-handling chapters in *Beyond Catch & Release*.

I have already mentioned **Paul Schullery** and his peerless credentials as an angling historian. Although I've never been well acquainted with Mr. Schullery, after I rang him up last summer and bleated for help, he was unstintingly generous with his assistance and advice on the historical portions of this book. It is a far better book because of him, and I thank him deeply.

Ted Leeson, another friend and colleague from my magazine days, provided invaluable advice on the "etiquette" sections of *Beyond Catch & Release*. Not only did he help add many nuances to what I had written about onstream courtesy and ethics, but his assistance with some suggested "rules of the rowed" for driftboat skippers was indispensable. Unlike Ted, who is a veteran navigator of such crowded aquatic combat zones as Montana's Madison River, I myself am not an oarsman. Thank you, Ted.

Dr. Robert Behnke, widely and deservedly credited with being the world's foremost scientific authority on trout and salmon, provided me with some good insights into the effects of water temperatures on trout. I greatly appreciate his help—and I still have a very fond memory of having fished with him from a canoe in Colorado years ago. We caught some very nice cutthroats that day. Like Nick Lyons, Dr. Behnke is the finest in his field, and likely will never be replaced.

Steve Kantner, Florida's esteemed "Land Captain," was kind enough to research the "Vulcan death grip" for me. Steve himself prefers the less-exotic technique of turning a snook or other saltwater fish onto its back in order to immobilize it for hook removal.

Along with the people who helped directly with *Beyond Catch & Release*, I also must mention a few who have had an indirect, though still important, influence on this book. **Amedio "Ham" Gallipoli** is the former Milford, Connecticut, firefighter who first placed that fly rod in my hands all those years ago; thank you, Ham.

After I'd moved to Maine, **Leslie "Deek" Crowley** was one of my first mentors in the practice of catch-and-release, as well as the man who repeatedly cajoled me into attending Kennebec Valley Trout Unlimited meetings until I finally started showing up and sticking around on my own. I'm grateful he didn't give up on me.

Of the many good things that came to me as a result of belonging to such a remarkable TU chapter, one of the most valuable was the education in the lives of rivers that I received from **Steve Brooke** during his many patient, thorough, and passionate reports concerning our progress in the long battle to get the Edwards Dam removed from the Kennebec River in Augusta. When KVTU and its allies won that fight, the victory inspired lovers of fish and rivers all across the country.

Three other KVTU members, **Richard Corbett**, **Sean McCormick,** and **Jim Thibodeau**, all in their own—and in at least one case, extremely unconventional—ways opened my eyes to different aspects of my home waters.

Joan Wulff was not my first casting instructor, but she certainly was my most determined one. For many years, whenever I dared make my way to the casting pool at a fly-fishing show, it would not be long before I would see, from the corner of my wincing eye, Joan swooping in like a diminutive fly-casting valkyrie, on a mission to obliterate my many faults in form. Thank you, Joan; not only did you make me a better caster, but a better angler overall.

I also owe thanks to all my many, mostly anonymous **minute mentors**. A fitting representative would be the tall, cultured-looking older gentleman I ran into on the banks of Willowemoc Creek one evening very long ago. He listened patiently and with an indulgent smile on his face as I, half-crazed with the mostly accidental success I'd been having, prattled on about my exploits. When I had finally exhausted my stock of inadvertent comedy material and asked him a presumptuous question about his own tactics that night, he hesitated for just a moment before apparently deciding that the most useful thing he could do for me was to leave me with my high spirits and exaggerated

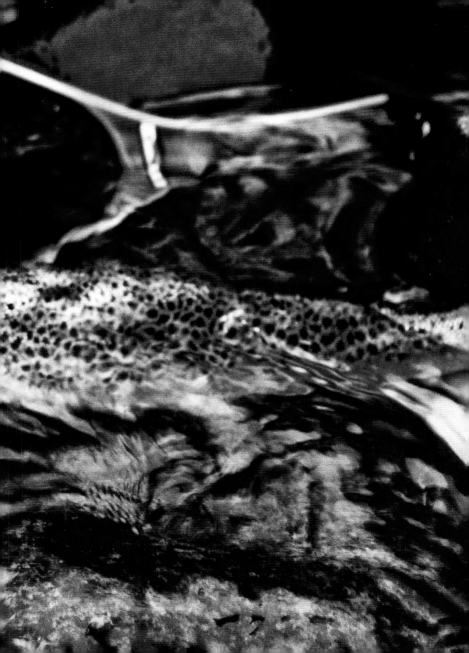

self-regard totally intact. He said, "You are absolutely correct. I caught them all on a *big* Adams."

Lastly . . . in this book I talk a great deal about good anglers, ethical anglers, anglers whom others look up to. The person I imagined most whenever I was writing such words was the late **Gary LaFontaine**. Although I was a mature adult when I first met him—perhaps even graying a bit by then—he's still one of the best role models I've ever had, or whom anyone could ever have had. I miss him.

—*Paul Guernsey*

Conservation Organizations

American Rivers
> 1101 14th Street NW
> Suite 1400
> Washington, DC 20005
> 202-347-7550
> www.americanrivers.org

American Rivers is the leading conservation organization standing up for healthy rivers so communities can thrive. American Rivers protects and restores America's rivers for the benefit of people, wildlife, and nature. Founded in 1973, American Rivers has more than 65,000 members and supporters, with offices in Washington, D.C. and nationwide.

The Atlantic Salmon Federation
> PO Box 5200
> St. Andrews, New Brunswick
> Canada E5B 3S8
> 506-529-4581
> www.asf.ca/

ASF works to protect and restore wild Atlantic salmon and their habitat.

California Trout

870 Market Street, Suite 528
San Francisco, CA 94102
www.caltrout.org

As the name suggests, CalTrout is an organization dedicated to protecting California trout, salmon, and steelhead and their habitat.

Coastal Conservation Association

6919 Portwest, Suite 100
Houston, TX 77024
713-626-4234
www.joincca.org

The CCA informs the public on issues related to the conservation of marine resources, with the goal of conserving those resources for the future.

Federation of Fly Fishers

PO Box 1688
Livingston, MT 59047
406-222-9369
www.fedflyfishers.org

The FFF is a "43-year-old international nonprofit organization dedicated to the betterment of the sport of fly fishing through conservation, restoration, and education. The Federation of Fly Fishers and its Councils are the only organized advocate for fly fishers on a national and regional level." The organization is divided into fifteen regional councils, plus a national office. One of the FFF's specialties is in training and certifying fly-casting instructors.

Greater Yellowstone Coalition

P.O. Box 1874
Bozeman, MT 59771

406-586-1593

www.greateryellowstone.org

Dedicated to protecting the lands, waters, and wildlife of the greater Yellowstone ecosystem.

The Nature Conservancy

4245 North Fairfax Drive

Suite 100, Arlington, VA 22203-1606

www.nature.org

Superb international organization that specializes in purchasing and/or otherwise protecting critical lands and waters. They usually welcome anglers onto property they have preserved.

Theodore Gordon Flyfishers

PO Box 2345

Grand Central Station

New York, NY 10163-2345

www.tgf.org

TGF is a New York–based angling and conservation organization.

Trout Unlimited

1300 N. 17th St.

Suite 500

Arlington, VA 22209-2404

www.tu.org

TU is a nationwide organization whose more than 150,000 members are dedicated to coldwater fisheries conservation and restoration. Every angler should belong to one of the more than four hundred Trout Unlimited chapters.

Oceana

www.oceana.org

Oceana, founded in 2001, is the largest organization dedicated specifically to ocean conservation.

The Wild Salmon Center
Jean Vollum Natural Capital Center
721 NW Ninth Ave., Suite 300
Portland, OR 97209
503-222-1804
www.wildsalmoncenter.org

The Wild Salmon Center is dedicated to protecting the remaining wild salmon ecosystems of the Pacific rim. The organization has done a great deal of exciting work on the Kamchatka Peninsula in the Russian Far East.

For Further Reference

Behnke, Robert J. *Trout and Salmon Of North America.* New York: The Free Press, 2002.

Burke, Monte. *"Who Fly Fishes?: Tom Brokaw." Fly Rod & Reel,* July/October 2003: 32-33.

Karas, Nick. *Brook Trout.* New York: Lyons & Burford, 1997.

Kerasote, Ted. *Heart of Home.* Guilford, Connecticut: The Lyons Press, 2003.

Leeson, Ted. *Inventing Montana.* New York: Skyhorse Publishing, 2009.

Leopold, Aldo. *A Sand County Almanac.* New York: Oxford University Press, 1949.

Plunket-Green, Harry. *Where the Bright Waters Meet.* London: Andre Deutsch Limited, 1983.

Posewitz, Jim. *Beyond Fair Chase: The Ethic and Tradition of Hunting.* Guilford, Connecticut: Morris Book Publishing, 1994.

Reiger, John F. *American Sportsmen and the Origins of Conservation, Third, Revised and Expanded, Edition.* Corvallis, Oregon: Oregon State University Press, 2001.

Schullery, Paul. *American Fly Fishing: A History.* New York: The Lyons Press, 1987.

Schullery, Paul. *Fly-Fishing Secrets of The Ancients.* Albuquerque: The University of New Mexico Press, 2009.

Schullery, Paul. *Searching For Yellowstone.* Boston: Houghton Mifflin Company, 1997.

Schullery, Paul. *If Fish Could Scream: An Angler's Search For The Future Of Fly Fishing.* Mechanicsburg, Pennsylvania: Stackpole, 2008.

Sholseth, Thomas J. *How Fish Work.* Portland, Oregon: Frank Amato Publications, 2003.

Stolz, Judith, and Judith Schnell (Eds.). *Trout.* Harrisburg, Pennsylvania: Stackpole Books, 1991.

Topping, Rhea. *Rod Rage: The Ultimate Guide to Angling Ethics.* Guilford, Connecticut: The Lyons Press, 2004.

Van Put, Ed. *Trout Fishing in the Catskills.* New York: Skyhorse Publishing, 2007.

Walton, Izaak. *The Compleat Angler.* Edited by G. Bethune. New York: Wiley and Putnam, 1847.

Waterman, Charles F. *A History of Angling.* Tulsa, Oklahoma: Winchester Press, 1981.

Williams, Ted. *Something's Fishy: An Angler Looks at Our Distressed Gamefish and Their Waters—and How We Can Preserve Both.* New York: Skyhorse Publishing, 2007.

Wulff, Lee. *Lee Wulff's Handbook of Freshwater Fishing.* New York: Frederick A. Stokes Company, 1939.

Index

Field Notes

Field Notes

Field Notes